Loving Reminders for you.

Betty Lue

Dedication

I honor the great gift of being known and loved, always and all ways. I fully appreciate begin seen, from conception, as a gift of Love from God.

And so it is natural that I delight in giving this Sacred Gift of Loving Reminders to my world and my global family.

Every word I write to you in this way is a creation of Love.
I pray and consciously dedicate these writings to make a positive difference in your life and mine, to facilitate the awakening.

May these words written and thought awaken all humanity
to remember our True nature,
that of Love and Goodness and Beauty.

Betty Lue

Loving Reminders

A Practical Guide
to Everyday Spirituality

By Betty Lue Lieber, Ph.D.

Copyright © 2000
by Betty Lue Lieber, Ph.D.

All rights reserved. No part of this book may be reproduced in any form without the written permission from the publisher.

Reunion Press
17664 Greenridge Road
Hidden Valley Lake, CA 95467
(800) 919-2392

First Printing 2000
ISBN: 0-9706315-0-2

Reprint 2013
ISBN: 978-0-9899133-0-0

Acknowledgments

Loving Reminders come from my quiet Mind and Open Heart, where I listen to the Voice Within, the Spirit of Wholeness, that lives within each one of us.

You, the readers, have been my inspiration, my reason, and my encouragement for putting them into book form.

My Godsent Life Partner, Robert Waldon, is my helpmate and supportive friend in bringing the printed form to you with spiritual integrity.

I am forever grateful to the Love that lives within me and sets me free to totally trust in the Love We Are together.

Thanks to all of you who recognize and honor this Love.

Introduction

Loving Reminders are written **for me.** Usually early in the morning when I am not travelling, I sit down and write whatever comes to me. There is no hesitancy or forethought, but rather a spontaneous pouring forth of whatever I am called to write. For a gift to be wholly received spiritually, it must be fully received by the messenger. So I take time to receive it for myself and sometimes correct the typos.

I know that everything is perceived through the filters of the recipient. Therefore I trust that you will interpret what you read through your own beliefs, judgments and life experience. Together we are exploring our world and the integration of spiritual principles in everyday life. We are bringing heaven to earth. We are 'folding in the egg whites to lighten the cake' of life. Each one of us, co-creator and chef, we make heavy or make light. We can make the spiritual food inviting and delicious or forced and bland.

I am with you individually and collectively because I am You. You each represent a part of me that seeks to love and be loved. You show up in my life as teacher and learner, so I can learn what I am teaching and see in you what I have learned. The mirror can be directed in many ways for me to see mySelf, my Greater Self, my Holy Self, my One Self in all its many facets and personalities and bodies and missions.

I know You as I know mySelf. I love and respect You as I love and respect my Self. Any place where there is resistance or doubt, there is fear. Fear is not real, being easily dissolved by Love. I am given to write and speak in order that I might better know the Love I Am, which is All of us together.

I have great respect and gratitude for you!

Betty Lue

Pledge of Love

I pledge to give all of my Being to Love.
In trust and freedom I experience Love.
I express Love. I am Love.

I pledge to respect all beings,
to honor all paths,
to reverence all creation as sacred.

I commit my Self to be the Love I am,
to share the abundance I receive,
to offer the Truth I know,
to bring the Joy I experience.

I pledge to always remember the Source
from which all things come;
to be grateful for the joy of being here,
to facilitate our spiritual family-community
in the co-creation of a New World,
the Real World,
Heaven on Earth.

Always a Learner

I am an Eternal Student, a Lifelong Learner, an observer of people and events, a philosophical researcher, an adventurer in life, a playful experimenter.

I choose to be obvious in my learning and teaching, my observations and philosophical conclusions, until I learn differently. Then I will publicly and obviously change, undo, forgive and choose again.

I seek a better way. I am open to finding the best ways to awaken all of us to thoroughly enjoy the Abundant life we have. I delight in discovering ways to joyfully give All to All.

I learn as I write these Loving Reminders. I learn as I care for and play with my granddaughter. I learn by moving. I learn with the weather changes. I learn in every encounter. I learn as I travel. I learn easily because I am open and willing to seek the light and love of God and Good in everyone and everything. I am a happy and willing learner.

To Remember Who You Really Are

Are you willing to release the past?

Are you willing to unlearn limiting beliefs?

Are you willing to be Whole and Happy and Free?

Are you willing to trust in Spirit or a Higher Power?

Are you willing to take responsibility for your life?

Are you willing to extend love to all creation?

Are you willing to recognize you are teaching and learning with everyone?

Are you willing to give and receive abundantly?

Are you willing to experience inner peace?

Are you willing to commit to Self-Actualization?

Betty Lue Lieber, PhD, MFT

CONTENTS

Acknowledgments	v
Introduction	vi
Pledge of Love	vii
Always A Learner	viii
Dedication	ix
To Remember Who You Really Are	x
On Purpose	1
Ask And You Shall Receive	2
All Is A Call To Love	3
University of Love	4
All As One	6
Build A Better World	7
Answer The Call	8
Chooser or Loser	10
Pictures In Our Minds	11
Life Can Be Fun, Safe and Easy	12
Plow Your Own Field	13
Freedom To Experience	14
Choice, Change and Commitment	15
Unlimited Energy	16
Keeping Myself Full	17
Excuses, Excuses, Excuses	18
Do The Work	19
Changing Your Perceptions	20
Pleased With Your Life?	22
You Are Captain	23
Clearing Negativity	24
Preferences	26
No One Knows, But You	27
Willing To Let Go	28
Forgiveness Is A Gift	29
Spiritual Assessment	30
Creating A Spiritual Life	31

When To Move On	32
Choose	33
Fun, Safe and Easy	34
Learning From Our Children	35
The Real Work	36
The Mind	37
Enjoy The Process	38
Be A Happy Willing Learner	39
Forgiving The Past	40
Let Spirit Within Do The Work	41
Honoring Our Differences	42
The Gift You Are	43
When Others Criticize You	44
Improve On Perfection?	45
The Garden	46
Love Created Us As Love To Give Love	48
You Are Always Right Where You Need To Be	49
Our Own Natural Speed	50
Investments	51
Healing Is	52
Forgiveness	53
Open and Willing	54
Spiritual Prescription	55
Giving and Taking	56
Remember Who You Are	58
Our Essence	59
Ego and Spirit?	60
Challenges And Difficulties	62
Stating The Obvious!	63
Keep Your Agreements	64
How Do You Know You Are Loved?	66
Love	67
Interconnected	68
Circle of Influence	69

I Forgive	70
Your Best Self	72
Love No Matter What	73
In Faith	74
Detachment	75
Tired of Being Tired?	76
Living On Purpose	77
Love Is The Answer	78
Time For Action	79
Real Relationships	80
Judgment Gets You Stuck	81
The Truth About Real Relationships	82
Are You Ready?	83
Freedom	84
Love Is Freedom and Trust	85
Keep Your Life On Track	86
Created To Create	87
Golden Rule	88
Giving	89
To Heal Myself	90
Peace Must Come First!	91
Beliefs	92
What I Believe	93
Consciousness	94
Be Here Now	95
Introvert or Extrovert?	96
Be Unique! Be You!	97
All Are Chosen	98
Polish Your Diamond	99
Thoughts Create	100
Affirmations	101
Prayer	102
Prayer For A Loved One	103
Your Mind Is Like A Television	104

Life and Death	106
Saying "Good-Bye"	107
Giving Thanks	108
Hope: Happiness Overcomes Past Experiences	109
Charity and Contribution	110
How Do You Like To Be Loved?	111
30 Days To Enlightenment and Freedom	112
Spiritual Tips for Abundant Living	113
Living On Purpose	114
Death and Dying	115
Keys to Conscious Creation	116
Enjoy The Show	117
Negative Thinking	118
Seeing	119
Ingest the Best and Forget the Rest	120
Let Go	121
When The Path Becomes Difficult	122
Learning To Trust	124
What's Right?	125
Yours To Do	126
You Know What Is Best	127
Feeling Down	128
Loving You	129
Freedom and Trust	130
Prayer For Remembering	131
Reminding You	132
Realize The Love	133
Effective Clearing	134
Are You Willing	135
Never Quit	136
Choose Love Instead of Fear	137
Afraid of Not Being Loved	138
Saying "Thank You"	139
Follow Your Heart	140

Never Too Late!	141
Giving and Getting	142
You Are The Gift	143
How Love Looks, Speaks and Acts	144
Love Is	146
Life Is Working	147
Being Responsible	148
Upsets	150
What We Sow, We Reap	151
It's About Time!	152
The Game of Life	153
Listening	154
How Do We Know?	155
Be Authentic	156
Touch Someone	157
Anger	158
Everything Matters	160
Trust In Good	161
Philosophy of Life	162
Beliefs Made Real	163
Love and Gratitude Are The Giving Way	164
Generosity and Tithing Are The Teaching Way	165
Life Is A Garden	166
Life Is a "Fail-Safe" Learning Laboratory!	168
Is Love Special?	169
One	170
Led By Your Inner Voice	171
Divine Love or Human Love	172
What If?	174
Are You Awake	176
Enlightenment Is Now	177
Love No Matter What	178
Simple Truths to Remember	179

Betty Lue Lieber, PhD, MFT

On Purpose?

How do we know when we are "off purpose"?

How do we know when life is "working" and "not working"?

How do we know what is meaningful and fulfilling?

How do we know where we are to be and what we are to do?

Sometimes pain or dis-ease tells us there is a conflict of interest within. It may seem like we have two points of view vying for attention. Sometimes there is confusion and distraction within. This may indicate we are unclear, unfocused and indecisive, perhaps easily tempted by the customary and usual path. Sometimes there is lethargy and lack of energy. Usually we are drained by spreading our thoughts and our activities too thin and lose energy with a sense of overwhelm. Sometimes we feel depressed or anxious, indicating fear of making the wrong choice and so avoiding any change or new direction. Sometimes we simply feel stalled or blocked in moving ahead. Probably we are being called to wait and get clarity before moving forward.

You probably have discovered your own indicators of needing to **"stop, look and listen"**. **Stop** what you are doing. Don't try to keep going when stressed. Take time for yourself.

Look at what you are experiencing, what you know, what you believe, and what you value. **Listen** to your own heart and mind for inspiration and inner direction. Listen within..

You are the greatest gift and guide in your own life.

Ask and You Shall Receive

When I sat quietly this morning I asked, "What do you want me to know?" and received the following:

You are beloved of the One Who is Your Source.

You need not search for knowledge, fame or glory.

Your connection with the Infinite is All You Need.

You need not write books, but rather Be what is written.

You need not build Centers of healing and growth, but rather be a Center of Trust and Freedom.

To live the Truth is far greater than any book or building.

Should you feel inspired to write and share in other ways, follow your joy.

Live only in the path of delight, for such is your calling.

You are the ultimate giver as you joyfully live.

The Truth is freely given in One who lives the Truth.

This is your gift to YourSelf and your world.

Let Forgiveness be your path.

Let Love light your way.

Let Joy be your guide.

Let Peace be your destination.

All is a Call to Love

I may be a dreamer.
If love begins within each one of us,
let it begin within ME and YOU!
Let this circle of love, respect, gentleness
and reverence begin in our homes.
Let this loving kindness begin as we live
in balance with nature.
Let us provide food and shelter
and Love to those who seek our help.

If everything has a purpose,
maybe every request for help is our personal responsibility.
Maybe our inner voice knows
exactly what and when and where to give.
Maybe our heart wants to share
and our mind doesn't let us care.
Maybe the One we give to
is just a reflection of our scared and lonely Self.
Maybe our fear will disappear,
when we know someone will always be there for us,
Because we are always there for others.

Betty Lue Lieber, PhD, MFT

University of Love

We are all attending the University of Love
and life is our learning laboratory.
Every relationship is our experimental assignment.
We are practicing the art of Love and Loving.
We are exploring and discovering
what works and what doesn't work.
We are willing to teach and learn together,
sometimes cooperatively and sometimes alone.
Each of us has a special area to explore,
a mission, a place to heal or understand.

Some of the signs of our successful learning are:
We learn to see the holiness and wholeness
 beneath apparent sin and separation.
We see an aspect of ourSelves in the other,
 a reflection of our perfection or our pain.
We remember how to love as God loves,
to Love with freedom and trust.
We bring the quality of holiness into our special relationships as we see beyond the human error.
We transcend the place of our own neediness
and bargaining to get something from someone.
We move into the space of sharing our Love
and our connection with Spirit with another.

We realize in all our relationships that to "respect" is to "look again" and see the goodness in the other.

We understand unloving behavior or unkind words

are always a cry for help, a call for love.

We answer every call for love with the listening, compassion and spiritual help we would like to receive.

We seek to understand the other's needs first,

before acknowledging our own.

We keep ourselves in a state of spiritual fitness,

so we are ever-ready to forgive and respond with love.

We never quit on Love or Loving.

We rejoice and celebrate every loving interaction.

Each relationship you have received is your assignment.

When you have succeeded, you will be given others.

Until we learn to love no matter what, there is more practice for us.

To Love Unconditionally is its own reward.

Graduation is inner peace!

All as One

While it seem we are all separate beings experiencing our own unique problems, triumphs, challenges and successes, we really are all individuated parts of a greater whole. We can see ourselves as a unified whole organism, a Spirit Being. When we function well with every cell performing its part perfectly, we are totally healthy and at peace. When any part begins to have difficulties, all other parts are affected.

So I am responsible for the greater Whole. I am here to offer my best Self to work in harmony for the Good of All.

If any one person in a family is sick, is not the whole family impacted and even at risk of getting sick? If any one in a community is homeless, are not all parts of the community involved? If any one in a company is cheating or stealing from the organization, is not the whole business directly affected?

When I function separately, I find safety in self-sufficiency. When I function as part of a team, I am interdependent with the others who are part of that team. And when I know I am part of the human family, living together on the Earth,, I know my thoughts, words, and deeds directly impact the greater Whole.

I am willing to contribute my best to the whole.

Build a Better World

Can you imagine a world without fear,
> a world of safety and of peace?

Can you imagine a world without hunger,
> where we feed all our brothers?

Can you imagine a world without harm,
> where we treat all with respect and gentleness?

Can you imagine a world with no disease,
> where we live in balance with nature?

Can you imagine a world with no homelessness,
> where everyone has shelter and a home?

Can you imagine a world of respect for our differences,
> where everyone is equally important?

Can you envision a planet of reverence for all life,
> where violence and killing are no more?

Can you foresee a place where everyone is cherished,
> the young and old, healthy and disabled?

You can help create a community of trust and freedom.

Your attitude, your voice and your choices can build a better world for All!

Answer the Call

How do you serve when there is a call for help?

How do you respond to stories of sorrow or terror?

What do you give when someone asks for some money?

Elder friends who feel uncertain and limited in life choices, grown children who experience life challenges, the skinny woman asking for a handout to buy gas everyday in the same parking lot, a dear friend who is still not well enough to work, the request in the mail for a contribution for a worthy cause, the political call to vote in the next primary, and my granddaughter's plea, "Pick me up, please".

Are they not all the same?

Everyone is calling for the affirmative prayer, "All is well."

Every call is seeking my willingness

    to respond with LOVE and TRUST.

Each individual is asking for my smile,

    my love, my support, my compassion.

When I am centered in absolute Trust and a willingness to LOVE no matter what, those who come to me receive the conscious message of my thoughts, my words, and my actions.

I am at peace.

I have remembered Love and returned to wholeness and Holiness.

I have given the best I know in my heart.

There are opportunities everyday to pray, to contribute, to lift up, to inspire, to help, to serve, to listen, to share, to offer, to travel, to give all you are and all you have been given.

I own nothing, and I have been given everything by my Source and Creator.

Therefore, I am here to Give All to All.

In so doing I have given to mySelf.

REMEMBER LOVE AND RETURN TO WHOLENESS

Betty Lue Lieber, PhD, MFT

Chooser or Loser

It is time to begin again.

It is time to sing a new song.

It is time to be renewed in Spirit.

It is time to step forward in our new choices.

It is your choice:

To trust where you have doubted.

To create where you have destroyed.

To forgive where you have condemned.

To believe where you have been disappointed.

To love where you have resisted.

To choose where you have been victimized.

To laugh where you are afraid.

To find what you are seeking.

To accomplish what you have been attempting.

To do what you have put off.

To learn what you have wished for.

To have what you have envied.

To hope where you have given up.

You can be a chooser or a loser.

Life works for those who choose and persist in their choices. Those who wait for someone else to choose get whatever may be left.

Pictures in Our Minds

What we see comes from our own inner projections!

The pictures we hold in our minds create what we perceive.

First, we believe and then we see that which we believe.

Life is the opposite of what we think.

Experience follows thought.

What we want to be true is what is true for us.

We then seek others to agree to validate our self-made "truth".

It is all "made up"!

The world we see is merely our dream or nightmare.

Objective reality is really a subjective projection on the movie screen of life.

We give everything we see the meaning it has for us.

Changing our mind changes our life.

We are responsible for everything that happens to us, for we have asked for it.

To be totally responsible for our life experience is the greatest power we have.

To resist responsibility creates the greatest pain and suffering we can know.

Forgive and trust.

Live and learn.

Appreciate and let go.

Be willing to really "see" beneath the apparency.

Life Can Be Fun, Safe and Easy

Interpretations will vary according to which part of ourselves is in charge.

The ego's interpretation may be to seek pleasure and comfort and ease. This often leads to selfishness, lethargy and laziness.

The ego, wanting to avoid hardship, becomes gluttonous.

The ego, wanting to avoid pain, becomes careful.

The ego, wanting to avoid work, becomes lazy.

This is the downfall and demise of humanity.

Spirit's interpretation is to enjoy life, stay in love and follow your heart's desires.

This leads to full appreciation and delight,

the recognition of 'no harm", and a life of boldness

and courage, challenge and adventure.

Spirit appreciates the gift and blessing in everything.

Spirit knows the apparency of harm can be forgiven and wholeness restored.

Spirit honors the inner call which directs and guides our lives to be lifted up.

Thus the Inner Spirit of each one will provide a life that is truly fun, safe and easy!

FUN is joyfully giving the abundance of Love we are.

SAFE is trusting in the Highest Good for everyone.

EASY is daring to follow the calling of our Spirit.

Plow Your Own Field & Plant Your Own Corn

Are you minding our own business?

In the name of love, we often busy ourselves with another's business. We scrutinize, compare, evaluate and even tell others what we think of their life choices. We would do better tending to our own garden. We must plant the seeds for our own destiny and care for our own intentions and creations. After we have achieved success and happiness for ourselves, we can share our experiences and insights with confidence, when asked for help or advice.

How often the expert's bed is unmade, their checkbook not balanced, their family in disharmony, their health in jeopardy, and their lives unfulfilled. And to feel better about themselves, they criticize someone else. Parents, bosses, leaders, and advisors need to teach by example. Authority figures need to put their own house in order. Elders must be self-respecting to be respected. We all can practice better what we preach and teach. You and I have no right to judge another, when we are still working on ourselves.

We all have a garden of possibilities to tend. We have a life to lead and a job to do. For each one of us, our life garden is our primary responsibility.

I am working on my garden every day.

Freedom to Experience

Under stress, we either become more analytical and picky or we become more generalizing and global. To be both creative and practical, we need both working together.

Fear seems to force our mind to go for its strength. Those who are discerning, judging, and scrutinizing become even more so. Those who are creative, expansive, seeing the big picture become even more so. The judging folks slow way down and get caught in each detail. The creative folks become scattered and lose their focus.

We can decrease our stress and fear by reassuring ourselves that mistakes are opportunities to learn. We can minimize our stress by looking at how we would handle the mistakes that may come up. We can reduce our stress by trusting in the perfect outcome, no matter what might happen. We can actually enjoy the whole experience by courageously choosing to be a risk-taker and enjoy the consequences of our choices, right or wrong, good or bad.

To be alive is to experience stress and uncertainty.

To be free is to expose ourselves to both success and failure.

To be strong is to trust in a Higher Power for guidance.

To be clear we can honor our intuition and inner voice.

To be honest is to know we learn from our errors.

To be loving is to accept whatever may happen.

Choice, Change and Commitment

These are your "power tools" for life.

What do you choose for today?

Remember your power is in your intention.

Choose for the Highest possibility.

 Hold your course.

What are you changing today?

Know you hold the steering wheel.

Dare to change direction when you are off course.

Where are you committed?

Commit to what has heart and meaning for you.

Give your All to where you want 100% success.

By choosing to clarify your intention, changing what no longer works, and committing to what you wholeheartedly desire, you cannot fail.

I choose to live fully and love freely.

I easily change my mind when I forget.

I commit to be a loving reminder.

Unlimited Energy

Folks sometimes question, **"How can you do so much?"**

I respond, "With Spirit, I am willing to give all I have."

It takes no energy to keep going in the direction you have chosen.

It exhausts and depletes life energy to stop, to figure out,

to change direction, to doubt, to explain or justify behavior,

to be careful, to get agreement or permission.

With total commitment to inspired living and abundant giving:

One's energy keeps on flowing like a river in the constant direction of willingness to Love.

One's mind supports the choice to Love. It does not question or doubt the choice.

One's emotions are joyful and content to contribute wherever I am called.

The body is energized as I use it with love to share the Love I Am.

Finances are abundant as I give what I have to contribute to a better way for All.

Relationships are supportive and appreciative as I live what I teach.

I give my Self to Love today.

Keeping Myself Full

I must take exquisite care of myself physically, mentally and spiritually.

I must fully appreciate notes of gratitude and love.

I must respond to every question and listen to the blessing of its answer.

I must answer every phone call as though God were calling me.

I must prepare meals, do laundry and clean house for the Christ who visits.

I must enjoy what I do and do what I enjoy.

I must love myself in all ways with no criticism or complaints.

I must appreciate my past and look forward to my future.

I must surround myself with beautiful people, places and things.

I must turn away from negativity, violence, and regret.

I must turn toward delight, helpfulness and appreciation.

I must complete all the projects I begin or let them go with my blessing.

I must listen within for direction and guidance.

I must stand tall, think clear and live clean.

I must be All my Creator intended that I be.

Excuses, Excuses, Excuses

Too much laundry, too many phone calls, too many bills to pay we may say. Too little time, lacking in energy, not enough help or money, or just plain, "Nay".

"I don't want to and you can't make me."

"I don't feel like it, and besides what does anyone do for me?"

"Who cares anyhow? It won't be noticed."

"It doesn't matter!" "Maybe later, if I feel like it."

"Let's rest up first or maybe eat something."

"Let's watch TV or maybe finish my book."

Excuses simply limit you and shut out any creative possibilities. Figuring out how and when and why is merely a delaying tactic. Justifying your history or feeling sorry for yourself is an attempt to wait.

It is time to **DO THE WORK!**

Clean up your house and keep it clean every day.

Clear up your relationships and keep them clear.

Balance your life and keep it balanced with inspired and conscious living. Wake up and stay awake. There is no time to be lazy, if you really want Joy!.

Freedom comes from taking care of your distractions.

Inspiration comes from time for Spirit everyday.

Joy comes from changing your mind and your life.

So no more excuses.

Do The Work

What is your "work"?

Have you ever read a self-help book and not done the exercises?

Have you ever taken a personal growth workshop and put nothing into practice?

Have you ever gotten clear inner guidance and direction and forgotten what you heard?

Have you ever discovered a personal talent or gift and said, "Maybe I'll use it later in life?"

"The work" is to practice everyday what you are wanting to improve.

"The work" is to listen and follow everyday what you know inside.

"The work" is to roll up your sleeves and take action to move you in the direction you are seeking.

"The work" is to stop hoping and praying and waiting for something to change you and your life.

"The work" is to do the work you know needs to be done.

Ask yourself, "What three things could I begin now that would have the greatest impact on my life if completed?"

Do them NOW! This is your WORK!

Changing Your Perceptions

It is not up to you to change your brother!

To attempt to change someone else is to not appreciate who they really are.

To try to correct a brother is to attend to the error and not the perfection.

To focus on what is wrong begets more of what appears wrong.

To try to understand or to explain or justify another's mistakes makes them real.

What we see in another could not be seen

if we did not know it in ourselves.

How we interpret another's behavior leads to guilt and fear,

or forgiveness and love.

How we judge another holds what we have judged in place.

Seek to love. Let go of fear.

Seek to forgive. Let go of judgment.

Seek to trust. Let go of doubting.

Seek to see wholeness. Let go of imperfection.

Seek to set free. Let go of restrictions and rules.

Seek to encourage with appreciation. Let go of destruction and deprecation.

Seek opportunities for creating beauty. Let go of limiting full free expression.

You are more beautiful than you know.

Your brother is like unto yourself.

We all blossom in warmth and light.

So share your kindness and gratitude liberally.

And watch your relationships grow in beauty, goodness and holiness.

Joy comes from seeing the beauty and goodness and wholeness in One Another!

Pleased With Your Life?

Can you say that you are pleased with your home, pleased with your nutrition, pleased with your work, pleased with your family interactions, pleased with how you think, pleased with your gifts to your community? Respecting your life and yourself means giving your whole Self the finest and the best in all areas. Taking responsibility means assuming leadership in every relationship and situation. This means leading by example, not telling others what they should do to clean up your life! And Cooperation means that you begin being truly helpful everywhere and invite others to join you with enthusiasm and gratitude.

To create from your Spirit requires a willingness to relinquish attachment, to be free of distractions, detours and delays. To take care of business first frees you up to open to Spirit. To relinquish attachments you must let go of past limiting beliefs, habits, neediness and resistance. To let go of what is no longer of value requires a conscious choice to do the work!

The work is to stop, look, listen and let go!

Stop accumulating! Stop making excuses!

Look at what you have and what you have created.

Listen for what is valuable and what you really want!

Let go of all that no longer serves the Best You!

You Are Captain

Begin by asking key questions. Get clear about what you want.

Make lists about what you want to do, to have, and to be.

Stop following others. Listen to your Self.

Find your own values. Family, wealth, purpose, Spirit, health, achievement, security, partnership, love freedom, mastery?

Define your goals. Do the goals aligns with your values?

Make sure your lifestyle supports your values.

List everything you believe you need to achieve your goals.

Write down your first three steps and begin your action.

Do something everyday to support actualization.

Appreciate every supportive daily activity you choose.

Take time weekly to reevaluate your activities

Wherever not on target, change your attitude and activities.

Wherever you are on target, celebrate and do more.

You are the captain of your ship and the master of your own destiny.

How fulfilled we are and how great we become when living our own truth is our total responsibility!

Passion is the fuel

Vision is the compass.

Choice is the chart.

And you are captain at the helm!

Clearing Negativity

Do you ever imagine the worst?
Do you entertain harmful possibilities?
Do you ever prepare for a disaster?
Do you envision negative outcomes?
Do you consider experiences you don't want to have?

Remember, our thoughts create.
Faith, belief, and vision create.

When you visualize negative possibilities,
when you believe that bad things will happen to you,
when you have faith in undesirable outcomes,
you are literally unconsciously creating them.

Simply acknowledge and forgive your negative, protective mind.
Be reassuring, "Nothing bad is going to happen."
"Don't worry. It will all turn out OK somehow."
"It is time to believe in positive possibilities."
"Good things have happened before.
      They can and will happen again."
"I know what I really want.
      So I will plan on it and work toward it."
"Let us get creative and look for the highest possible outcome."
"Everything always works more exquisitely than I can plan."

Hope is always more motivating than despair.

Prayer works as we consider healing and miracles and divine intervention.

Wherever two or more are joined, there will be a collective consciousness that supports the chosen outcome, whether positive or negative.

Where there is only apparently one supporting the Good, there are many others in prayer and spiritual work who are always joined with every loving possibility.

Remember, fear works when we give it power to lead.

Why not choose for love instead?

I believe the consciousness of all humanity is now

awakening to the creative power of its own mind.

Preferences

I prefer workers over whiners and complainers.

I prefer those who do, rather than those who tell others to do.

I prefer the ones who ask to help rather than wait to be asked.

I prefer those who practice what they are learning by living it.

I prefer those who commit to something and accomplish it.

I prefer those who know what they want and choose it.

I prefer those who play as equals on the team of life.

I prefer those who accept total responsibility for their lives.

I prefer those who are always seeking to improve themselves.

I prefer those whose actions speak louder than words.

I prefer those who when asking for help or advice, appreciate and use what is given.

I prefer those who listen within and respect what they hear.

I prefer those who appreciate and affirm themselves.

I prefer those who are truly happy with their own lives.

I prefer those who look for what is working, not dwelling on what is wrong.

I prefer those who make immediate changes, when change is needed.

I prefer those who really listen with an open heart and mind.

I prefer those who keep their promises and agreements, with themselves and others.

What do you prefer? Are you living your own preferences?

No One Knows, But You!

What is your responsibility?

How does what you do in secret affect your whole life?

Do you ever leave litter behind for someone else to clean up?

Picnic area, the movies, a restrooms, a rental car, your hotel room, or in your kitchen? Are you teaching by example?

Do you ever take advantage of people who seem to have more than you? Take pens or paper clips, make personal phone calls, leave early from your workplace?

Are you teaching others to get away with as much as they can? Do you ever assume others' needs are taken care of so you need not offer your help? At church, clubs you belong to, a party you attend, a friend in the hospital?

Are you teaching others not to offer their help to you?

Do you ever judge someone by how they dress, what they say, their home or car? "Not like me", "too rich", a "know-it-all", "beneath me"? Are you teaching others to judge you by how you behave or the choices you make?

Do you ever get too busy to say thank you, to appreciate your friends and family? Be demanding, criticize, do 'important' things, forget to enjoy your life? Are you teaching others to forget to be grateful and respectful to you?

What you do in private teaches the world you live in!

Give your best in every moment and relationship!

Willing to Let Go

The more resistance and tension, the more pain.

The more we judge and avoid,

the more we increase and strengthen.

Some alternatives to resistance and judgment:

1) Step aside. Allow what is negative to flow on by.
2) Laugh and dispel the resistance.
3) Ignore or step away.
4) Deny what you do not like.
   "This doesn't matter." "This means nothing."
5) Erase your judgments.
   "I forgive my fear and release my resistance."
6) Breathe and allow it to be what it is.
7) Let go and let God.
8) Pause and take time out. Be patient and peaceful.
9) Observe yourself in the situation.
10) Appreciate and enjoy the experience.
11) Step inside the other's perspective and respond to the true need present.
12) Seek first to understand, then to be understood.

RESPOND WITH LOVE OR REACT WITH FEAR?

Make a new choice and release the stress, fear and negative pattern!

Forgiveness

Forgiveness is a gift to ourselves.

It offers us relief from anger and fear.

Forgiveness sets us free.

It alleviates the pain, the past, the wounded heart and mind.

Forgiveness softens our hearts.

We can reach out and love again.

Forgiveness opens our minds.

It allows us to see from another's viewpoint.

Forgiveness blesses the world we see.

Its function is to erase the errors in our world.

Forgiveness becomes our function in life.

Through our forgiveness, we can choose again.

We are free of the guilt and fear of past and future mistakes.

We can consciously look at all possibilities and listen within.

We can seek always for a better way to learn and love and live.

May we begin now to forgive everything and everyone.

May we seek to let go of the past and choose now for the most loving path.

May we know great peace, as we trust that only Love prevails.

Spiritual Assessment

Let's assess our own lives. Are we making the daily choices which serve our Best Self?

Ask yourself:

Am I strengthening myself with every activity of my day?

Am I living my values?

Am I giving to others what I really want myself?

Am I eating what is good for me?

Am I speaking words of wisdom, faith, hope and love?

Am I acting in ways which I respect?

Am I choosing friends who support my Best Self?

Am I living in a home which encourages me to feel happy & safe?

Am I giving my best where I work?

Am I reading and watching material which sustains inner peace?

Am I grateful for all I have?

Am I really happy with myself and my life?

We are responsible for our choices.

We are responsible for choosing to love ourselves.

We are responsible for respecting our need to honor our Highest and Best Self.

And where we have erred, we can forgive ourselves and choose again.

Creating a Spiritual Life

To freely create a spiritual life, first you must consciously manage your worldly life!

Clarify and write you own mission statement preferably using seven words or less.

Discover and list your top five chosen values. (Values are where you choose to devote your time, energy and resources)

Notice where you expend your time, energy and money. (What do you think about and talk about)

Make a list of the guiding principles which keep you on track and focus your life.

Balance your checkbook. Pay all your bills.

Keep an accurate ledger of all your expenditures.

Clean our your refrigerator. Release dead food and things that have not been used for a year, as well as food that is not supportive of your family's health.

Make a list of what you believe would be valuable for you and your family to eat.

Clean out your bathroom. Throw away all products not used in the last year. Throw away outdated and expired medications.

Notice what is difficult for you to do or release.

Notice where you are resisting, angry or afraid of DOING THE WORK!

When to Move On

How and when does one decide about moving, career changes, leaving the body, changing partners or lifestyles.

Let go when you are complete, fulfilled, neutral, at peace.

Otherwise, what is undone or unresolved will follow you.

Everything unhealed will come up for healing.

So when you are about to make a change,

make peace with everyone and everything.

Life is a failsafe learning laboratory.

Our unfinished work or unlearned lessons

keep coming back for our completion.

You will eventually forgive and erase it all, so why not now?

Where there are regrets, make amends.

Where there is blame, forgive.

Where there is disappointment, take action.

Where there is lack, contribute,

Where there is limitation, set free.

Where there is littleness, see the Gift.

Move on first with your attitude and loving heart.

Choose

Every moment is an opportunity to CHOOSE AGAIN for the life you really want!

Right now you can choose for the thoughts you want to think! Right now you can decide on the experience you want to have!

Why not use everything to wake up?

Why not take responsibility for your choices?

Why not sort out what you really want from what you don't?

Why not forgive and erase past unwanted choices?

Why not use everything for your good?

Why not trust yourself to learn from every experience?

Why not consciously choose what you really want to have?

Why not live and give exactly what you want every moment?

Why not appreciate yourself for taking the risk to choose consciously?

What do you really want right now?

Do you deserve it?

Are you willing to give it?

Are you ready to have it?

Why not right now?

You are the chooser, so why not?

Fun, Safe and Easy

Life will be totally safe when we have ceased all attack.

We must stop attacking ourselves and others.

Attack begets counter-attack.

Attack demonstrates fear.

Attack comes from a judgment that we are not safe.

To attack is to strengthen not being safe.

Judging indicates lack of understanding and acceptance.

Fear demonstrates lack of love and peace.

In our defenselessness our safety lies.

When we are trusting God within, we feel safe.

When we feel safe, we need not defend ourselves.

When we are not defending, we surrender to Love.

Fear and judgment demonstrate lack of Love.

All fear disappears when we choose to Love.

Love is Who we are. Love is the creative Power.

Love is the reason for our Being.

When we live in Love,
Remembering that Love is Who We Are,
Life is fun, safe, and easy.

Learning from our Children

There are so many jobs parents are trying to do.
What about the job of just being You!
Don't forget what our children can do.
They show us their job, when we don't have a clue.
Sing when you're happy and cry when you're sad.
Be bold and daring. Express when you're mad.
To handle emotions is to make sure
To have more good ones than bad. This is the cure.

Children love life's adventures.
They learn all the time.
They copy achievers.
They become true believers.
Children are flexible.
They do one thing at a time.
They like to do work to accomplish something important.
They try harder with encouragement.
They light up with praise.
They give up with discouragement.
They love freedom to grow and explore.
And they want someone nearby to love and adore.
Learn all their lessons by watching them play.
Life is their classroom. They learn their own way.
Let your children teach you about being you.

The Real Work

If Love is Who We Are, then maybe we are here to clean up everything that is not Love?

Our real life work and purpose is very simple:

Cleaning up our thoughts, our habits, our emotions.

Forgiving our memories, our relationships, our histories.

Plowing under our guilt, our resentment and our fears.

Recognizing and releasing all blocks to Being the Love We Really Are!

This is our Real Work!

So let us consciously and consistently commit to doing the Real Work of Life!

Let's together respectfully and responsibly join to release the false self and Remember Our True Identity.

Love is who You Are.

Love is who I Am.

There is nothing else to Know.

There is nothing else to seek.

There is no one else to be.

BE THE LOVE YOU ALREADY ARE.

The Mind

The mind is our creative engine, our image-maker. The mind generates ideas, perceptions, beliefs, attitudes, emotions, and experiences. It creates from the input it receives. When it receives garbage, it generates garbage. When it receives beauty and goodness, it generates goodness and beauty.

Static on the line interferes with our ability to hear and understand. So it is with the mind. When our creative and decision-making computer is filled with confusion, doubt, past history, defensiveness, meaningless chatter, plotting and planning for our chosen outcome, it is very difficult to access our Higher Inner Authority, where the guidance and direction are pure and perfect and always in our own best interest.

Quiet your mind with forgiveness, meditation, affirming prayer, visualizations, affirmations, inspiring words, and inner peace.

Clean out the garbage and clutter in your mind.

Fill your mind with light so it can really see.

Erase past experiences and limiting beliefs with forgiveness.

Welcome real and lasting happiness.

Let go of being harmed by anyone or anything.

Place your trust in your Inner Director.

Choose to listen to the Inner call, the Voice of Love.

Lead yourself to a light-filled life of trust and joy.

Free your mind of limitations, lack and littleness.

Decide for freedom, abundance and magnificence now.

Enjoy the Process

If life delivers what you really **don't** want, what do you do?

1) Take it with resentment?
2) Believe it belongs to you?
3) Imagine you deserve it?
4) Smile and pretend you like it?
5) Ask for something else?
6) Graciously refuse to accept it?
7) Deny it could possibly belong to you?
8) Give it to someone else?
9) Blame someone for giving it to you?
10) Take it and make it into something wonderful?

Our creations, the gardens in our lives, don't always give us what we may have thought we wanted. Perhaps we were unclear, or changed our mind, or had conflicting thoughts, or simply let someone else choose for us.

All experiences are truly opportunities to appreciate and celebrate, or opportunities to forgive and practice the art of simply choosing again. Such is the Divine learning plan.

Enjoy the process. It works when we do the work!

Be a Happy Willing Learner

I realize what makes my life truly fun, safe and easy is exactly this. I am here to learn actively consciously from everyone and everything every moment! I am willing and open to learn the High Truth, the Highest and Best all the time. I am happy and delighted with my new and renewed awarenesses.

Some loving reminders:

There is nothing NEW under the sun.

Yet everything seems new, as we remember "We are just One."

I know nothing; yet with inner connection, I know everything.

Life is an active teacher of what we think is true.

We are actively teaching with what we say and do.

I love being reminded of the Love We Really Are.

And I am willing to erase mistaken beliefs, and attachment to our false identity.

It feels lazy to excuse our mistakes with "I'm only human!"

I am a Spiritual Presence desiring to awaken humanity to our True Identity.

So how can I agree that I am limited and lacking and little?

Everyday I am challenged to exercise my choice and my free will to remember and lovingly remind my One Self of our Freedom, our Abundance and our Magnificence.

Choose what you want to be True for You.
Life is what you believe it to be!

Forgiving the Past

What if we remembered only the blessings of our past?

What if we forgave all seeming hurts and mistakes?

What if we erased everything not true and not genuinely loving?

What if we chose to accept that our parents always loved us?

What if the mistakes of our parents were from their past?

What if we really understood the stresses of our parents?

What if our memories were filled only with goodness?

What if our Dads gave us the kind of parenting they thought was best for us?

What if the time to return to unconditional love is now and we are the ones?

What if our right and responsibility is to forgive all mistakes of our forefathers?

What if our happiness depends on healing the past with our total forgiveness now?

What if our job is to love our parents differently than they loved us?

What if our fathers and mothers are released from guilt by our willingness to be whole, happy and free?

I know that forgiveness is the act of making whole and Holy

those relationships that may have been filled with fear and resentment and guilt.

And we are the Ones to give this precious gift of Love Now!

Be willing to love them all anyway!

Let Spirit Within Do the Work

How would I have my life be?

Am I willing to trust a Higher Power to lead me?

How can I let go of control and listen within?

Step back with a clean heart and an open mind.

Really let The Divine Within lead the way!

What is Your Will for me?

Where am I to go?

What am I to do?

What am I to say and to whom?

Begin practicing everyday conscientiously.

Learn to listen and follow.

The Way will be opened for you without your effort.

Acknowledge, "I am determined to see and hear and know Divine Will."

We are here only to clear all obstacles to the Path of Love.

When you are really free to listen and follow,

and when you have decided to trust in the one Power and Presence, you will know that **with Spirit there is no effort, only joy and ease.**

Honoring Our Differences

Are you less than others?   Are you more than others?

When you look around at your friends, family and global humanity, what do you see?

Are there those who seem not as fortunate, not as healthy, not as capable as you? Are those who seem richer, smarter, wiser and more loving than you? Are we created unequal or equal?

Are you really better than some and worse than some?

Are you created to be needy or abundant, sickly or healthy, meek or assertive? Are there "bad" babies and "good" babies?

What causes the apparent differences in people?

What helps and what hinders people in being their best?

Does it help to feel sorry, to pity, to sympathize, to commiserate? Does it help to look down, to ignore, to avoid, to give handouts? Does it help to worry, to reassure, to open your heart, to pray? Does it help to trust, to feel compassion, to feel grateful, to bless?

What would encourage and support you in being healthy, wise, abundant, and happy? How do you help others to develop their potential, to be their Best Self?

Give to others as you would have them give to you.

Respect and trust others as you want to be respected and trusted.

Honor and bless your brothers as you wish to be honored and blessed.

The Gift You Are

You are the gift.

In your healing, I am healed.

In your smiling, I find joy.

In your learning, I am filled with wisdom.

In your free expressions, I am empowered.

In your abundance, I too prosper.

In your spontaneity, I am set free.

In your joy, I know heaven.

And so it is that you give your Self to me

And I receive you with love and gratitude.

I am the gift I give to You

And I fully receive the gift I freely give.

As I know You, I know my Self.

As I give to you, I receive all good.

As I support you, I am supported by the Universe.

As I honor and respect you, I experience gratitude in all my being.

As I love you, I am loving all of God's creation.

I know you and believe in you.

I honor, respect and support you in being.

In you and me is all the Universe.

We are gifts to one another.

When Others Criticize You

You are never upset for the reason you think.

List what your mind makes up as cause:

"The real reason I feel upset is: .... "

Get to the heart of what can be sadness, anger, guilt, fear, relief, or hurt. Look for old feelings from many experiences in your lifetime (e.g. tears that were not cried or feelings that were not acknowledged.) "When you gotta let go, you gotta let go!" So do it. No more stuffing, no more emotional or spiritual constipation!

This is the time to let go of old patterns of self criticism and self doubt. You are doing the inner and outer work to set yourself free as God intended you to be. Only in personal freedom and perfect trust will you hear God's Will for you and know it to be true!

What others think of you and your choices is none of your business. Anyone can second guess and make up what God's Plan is in your life, because they aren't living their own.

When another is on course, living their inner calling, they will never judge your life choices.

Bottom line: As you live your own Life in integrity and peace, everyone in your life will be blessed. You lead the way. You demonstrate the courage and confidence to follow your heart. You are a shining example of a loving presence who recognizes and honors God's gift to You: Your Whole and Holy Self!

Improve on Perfection?

If you are a perfect expression of the Creator's Love, uniquely beautiful, good and whole, how could I dare to imagine that I know what is best for you?

As a parent, a friend, a counselor or teacher, how could I know your timing for growth, your ideal climate, your best care, let alone your potential for growth and beauty?

It sometimes feels like we are inexperienced **bonsai gardeners** who know nothing about anything, but still try to makeover, prune, add onto and undo what is not within our expertise. We place our limits, expectations, judgments and beliefs on others (and ourselves) without the slightest awareness of God's perfect plan for their happiness.

We think we can improve on what was created Perfect.

In our attempt to improve what isn't flawed or fix what isn't broken, we inadvertently create that which we have judged to be imperfect or in error.

I imagine that within each of us is the seed for our potential growth and healing. If nurtured, encouraged, celebrated and given the best possible climate and associations, the inner garden will blossom forth in beauty and splendor.

Oh! What a garden this world will be,

When each of us lives our possibility!

And you are here to set it all free

Just let your Self be all You can Be!

The Garden

You plant the seeds with your ideas, dreams and choices.

Your words (thought, spoken, or written) are the seeds.

Your consistent faith and focus provide water and nutrients.

Your gratitude, "This is good!", strengthens the harvest.

Your willingness to weed out limiting thoughts generates more bounty.

Your willingness to work the soil and renew the process creates more growth.

Your harvest offers the opportunity to choose again for the next planting.

Your blessing opens the way for more expansive seeding possibilities.

No one else can be the gardener in your life.

With no gardener your life will be dormant.

You must plant your own seeds or else weeds will grow.

All your words will create, so choose your seed words with care.

What you pay attention to, even what you don't want, will grow.

Condemning what you have grown in your life weakens your ability to choose well.

Sitting back and waiting for results after planting your seed ideas yields a meager harvest.

Spiritual laziness and not continually working the soil causes poor results.

Blessing your unwanted creations for their learning value and choosing again yields surprising success.

Judging and cursing your garden and the gardener leads to stagnation and suffering.

New beginnings with your next garden will be ever more beautiful, as you learn from every gardening experience and enjoy it all.

You cannot imagine the beautiful seeds planted in your soul until you are willing to **Do The Work!**

Plow the soil with forgiveness of the past.

Plant only seeds of goodness, wholeness and beauty in the present.

Water with focus and faith.

Weed out all unintended destructive and distracting thoughts and words.

Bless every aspect of the growth process.

Wait patiently and trust in the abundant harvest of your conscious living.

Celebrate and share the bounty with all who may benefit from your good works.

You can undo with love whatever you no longer want to harvest.

Begin again to choose your new garden today.

Love Created Us As Love to Give Love

Why would we ever choose to try to be anything else?

Forgetfulness?

Ignorance?

Copying others who are lost?

Being afraid of our Essence?

Following others?

Trying to learn about those who have forgotten?

Creating some alternative experiences?

Total foolishness?

How could I better support mySelf to be the Love I Am?

Total forgiveness of my past.

Daily loving reminders.

Affirmative thoughts and speech.

Helpful and loving activities.

Positive associations and friendships.

Loving visual and auditory input.

Treating my body, mind and Spirit respectfully.

Honoring Spiritual Truth.

Beauty in my environment.

Time spent in the wonder and mystery of nature.

Gratitude for the gift of life.

How can you remember to Honor the Love you Are?

You Are always Right Where You Need To Be

No matter what you choose, you will arrive at your chosen destination, if you keep going.

Some people become so discouraged by mistakes or hardships that they give up and quit on themselves. Some become self-doubting or distrustful when they believe they have made errors. Some are so comparative that anything less than the "best", any imperfect choice creates disappointment, guilt and regret. We could all lighten up on ourselves and others and learn to trust in the intrinsic "good", the opportunity to learn, beneath the apparency of a mistakes.

One man's obstacle is another person's reward. Maybe each one of us is playing the perfect part for others so that all of us arrive at our chosen destination together. Some are fast and some are slow. Some are farther along their path. Some have not begun yet. All of us will get where we are going in perfect time.

Everything always works more exquisitely than we can plan. Everything works together for good.

With forgiveness and non-judgment, the gift is received in every circumstance. Where there is love, there is always hope and charity. Everyone is always in the "right" place at the "right" time doing the "right" thing. There is really nothing to prove or defend, since **it is always all right!**

Our Own Natural Speed

We function best by giving ourselves the freedom to live according to our own energetic pace. I am noticing how much we influence and are influenced by those with whom we spend time. The rhythm of our speech, the pace of our gait, the rapidity of movements, our timing for putting our thoughts into actions; all of these are affected by our associations. Watch traffic flow, people pushing shopping carts, reading and writing speeds, the way some ponder and contemplate when answering questions. All of us need to live at our own pace, naturally and effortlessly flowing with our inner vibration.

When we stop to notice how others are being influenced by us, we collect dust (the judgments and "gazoobies" in life). One of the images that reminds me is how Jesus kept on walking. **To be proactive means to keep on moving in your chosen direction.**

When a spinning top slows down, it becomes wobbly or falls over. When I am moving naturally, every movement seems to easily open the way for the next without thought or judgment. I love my own natural flow and I trust you to find and enjoy your own.

Find your own rhythm.

Dance to your own drum.

Live in the precious present.

Enjoy your life exactly as you have created it to be.

Everyday is your creation.

Investments

Where are you investing your time, energy and resources?

What do you give your attention to?

Where do you put your thoughts and mental focus?

What calls forth your emotional intention?

What is the primary focal point of your physical energy?

In simple language, what do you do?

What do you talk about?

What do you feel passionately about?

And what do you ponder and contemplate?

Getting another's approval? Money? Avoiding conflict? Health? Aging? Getting a lot accomplished? Relaxing?

Finding pleasure? Saving? Friends? Helping others?

Getting through the day? Being the best? Comfort?

Keeping your marriage together? Learning more? Saving lives? Avoiding pain? Creating beauty? Food and meal preparation? Cleanliness and organization? Gratitude? Prayer?

Loving yourself?

World problems?

What else?

Where you invest, there will be your reward.

Healing Is

To heal is to make happy.

To heal is to remember our natural state of wholeness.

To heal is to be at peace.

To heal is to cease to use our body lovelessly.

To heal is to trust all is well.

To heal is to release all fear.

To heal is to forgive ourselves.

To heal is to open the flow of Love.

To heal is to be the Love We Are.

When we wish to heal something, to fix or change the "apparency", we want to change the outcome, the disease, the problem. In our effort to undo the " apparent mistake", we may actually judge, become afraid, and lock in that which we would like to let go. **What we give attention to grows and persists.** When we worry, our worries grow. We feed them with our consciousness. And when we are afraid or angry, we may actually stop the natural healing process. So let us forgive ourselves for judging and fearing. Let us choose listening, loving and trusting instead.

Offer peace where there is dis-ease.

Offer love where there is fear.

Offer light where there is darkness.

See the Truth beyond the apparency.

Hold the Peace and Love in our Mind no matter what.

Forgiveness

To forgive is to forget.

To forgive is to erase with love.

To forgive is to see things differently.

To forgive is selective remembering.

To forgive is to remember what is good and beautiful.

To forgive is to be willing to give love unconditionally.

To forgive is to love as God loves.

To forgive is to trust in the Abundance of Divine Love.

To forgive is to know acts of unlove are a call for Love.

To forgive is to recognize behavior is not the Being.

To forgive is to give Love to One Who has forgotten.

Jesus invited us to forgive seventy times seven. Any unloving or unconscious act is always a call for love, a call for forgiveness. The healing agent is our consistent willingness to forgive any and all acts of guilt, shame, vengeance, fear, and un-love. Each one of us is "healing inside out" our condemnation of envy, lust, betrayal, greed, control, manipulation, pain, neglect, denial, defensiveness, righteousness, arrogance, gluttony and more. "Damning" or "damming" the flow of love holds the seeming unloving act in place. Literally when Love has fulfilled itSelf we are free from the apparent "sin" or lack of Love.

Where Forgiveness is, the Light has come.

Darkness and fear have passed away.

Open and Willing

Every fear is an attack against yourself.

Every worry diminishes your flow of life energy.

Every judgment shuts the lens of your perception.

Every resentment hurts you.

Every criticism picks at yourself.

Every doubt lowers your confidence.

Literally what we think and say and do, both unconsciously and consciously, is given to ourselves.

We cannot give without receiving that which we have given.

We cannot impose our fears upon another without becoming more afraid ourselves.

What we perceive in another we strengthen in ourselves.

Maybe now is the time to listen to the messages of your heart and mind and voice.

Then ask yourself, "Is this coming from my fearful human ego or from my unlimited and loving Spiritual Essence? "

I choose to forgive and cancel all fear-based messages and beliefs.

My mind now automatically erases everything that is not wholly True and wholly Loving.

I am open and willing to listen to my inner guidance and follow the voice of Love and Trust.

Spiritual Prescription

When life feels hard, scary and too serious, you may want to have at hand a prescription from your Spiritual Doc. Try out these possible treatment measures and see what fits for you.

- Forgive and choose again.
- Breathe deep and trust.
- Give to someone.
- Be grateful for your life.
- Delight in the simple pleasures.
- Listen within and follow.
- Write loving reminders to someone.
- Ask God for help.
- Say "Thank You, God."
- Remember: "This too shall pass."
- Spend time alone.
- Take a walk.
- Let the trees comfort you.
- Invite the Light. "Light, Light, more Light."
- Sing or laugh out loud.
- Share with a real friend.
- Meditate.
- Affirm.
- Take a hot shower or soak in the tub.
- Clean your house or your car.

Put this somewhere handy in case of a spiritual urgency!

Giving and Taking

It is more blessed to give than receive. Is this true?

It is a blessing to receive. And to express gratitude is a gift to the giver. However most "takers" do not appreciate the gifts they receive. True "receivers" always give abundantly.

Some receive and forget to say "thank you". Some receive and make up that the giver needs to receive nothing in return. Some forget to say "thanks" because they are busy or distracted by life's challenges. Some have learned to "get" as much as they can, while giving as little as possible.

Some believe they have earned the " right to take" because they were deprived in childhood. Some feel they are worse off than others, so receiving is a way of "evening the score."

Some look around for a generous giver and asssume they have more than they need. Some maintain that they don't have the means or the energy to give. Some needy ones ask for more and complain when they don't get what they want.

Some takers feel like a bottomless pit, never fulfilled no matter how much is given. Some takers drain themselves with constant self judgment and hope for others approval.

Most "takers" are empty, lacking in confidence, dependent on others, scared they will never have enough, and insecure about their future.

It is a blessing to give. To give without conditions is the real gift.

Most givers have strings and expectations attached to their gifts.

True givers always give joyfully, and are fulfilled by the giving.

Some givers are rich and some are poor, but both are rich in desire to contribute.

Some givers want to have their gift received by a grateful receiver.

Some givers forget to enjoy the gift they give.

Some have learned to give it all away and feel depleted.

Some believe they should get a reward for their generosity.

Some feel obligated to give, since they have so much.

Some look for the most needy and bestow unwanted gifts.

Some feel limited in how much they can give and measure their giving.

Some give excessively and complain they are unappreciated.

Some givers feel arrogant and powerful in their controlling through giving.

Some givers are falsely motivated, and give for their own gain.

Sincere and joyful givers are guided by their inner Spirit and not their checkbook.

True givers receive the gift of giving themselves.

Giving is receiving.

True givers keep no accounting. They honor their inner Call, not the plea of the "taker".

True givers give to those who genuinely appreciate the gift given.

Remember Who You Are

Remembering Who You Are and the Purpose for Your Being is Your Responsibility!

This comes first, before right thought or action takes place.

What kind of world citizen are you?

What kind of minister, teacher, helper, mother, partner, friend, child are you?

Do you worry or do you trust?

Do you fear or do you love?

Do you demand or do you request?

Do you give up or do your best?

Do you need or do you give?

Do you really listen or hear what you want to hear?

Do you complain or are you grateful?

Are you light-hearted or heavy-handed?

Are you freeing or are you restrictive?

Are you flexible or controlling?

Are you forgiving or resentful and angry?

Do you resolve conflicts or carry grudges?

Do you try to "fix" others or see the "wholeness" beyond the apparent need?

Are you responsible for your life experiences or do you blame?

Is life fun, safe and easy for you or serious, dangerous and difficult?

Our Essence

Love is Who We Are

Freedom is the game.

Inner Trust is the Rule.

When our food is prepared with love, not thrown together and gobbled, we are free.

When our conversation is positive, and inspiring, not negative and alarming, we are free.

When our gifts are consciously selected, not carelessly purchased, we are free.

When our rest is plentiful and enjoyable, not uncomfortable and interrupted, we are free.

When our choices are preferences, not addictions, we are free.

When relationships are friendships, not dependencies, we are free.

When our work is play and not duty, we know we are free.

When our life is fun, safe and easy, not dreadful, dangerous and difficult, we are free.

We have free will to follow the freeway.

We can choose the side roads, detours, distractions and danger zones. Or we can smoothly and easily flow past the apparent obstacles, blessing them with our consciousness.

Ego and Spirit?

How can we tell which voice is directing us?
How do we know what to choose?
How do we deal with both parts of ourselves.

Ego questions.	Spirit affirms.
Ego doubts.	Spirit believes.
Ego discredits.	Spirit honors.
Ego denegrates.	Spirit respects.
Ego interprets.	Spirit knows.
Ego limits.	Spirit frees.
Ego compares.	Spirit admires.
Ego finds fault.	Spirit appreciates.
Ego separates.	Spirit joins.
Ego makes do.	Spirit visions.
Ego puts down.	Spirit lifts.
Ego deflates.	Spirit inspires.
Ego gives up.	Spirit calls forth.
Ego seeks a win.	Spirit seeks peace.
Ego serves itself.	Spirit serves All.
Ego conserves.	Spirit contributes.
Ego is selfish.	Spirit shares.
Ego is clever.	Spirit is wise.
Ego worries.	Spirit knows "All is well".

Ego explains.	Spirit see what is.
Ego defends and justifies.	Spirit tells the Truth.
Ego focuses on past & future.	Spirit is present.
Ego wishes.	Spirit creates.
Ego depends on others.	Spirit co- creates.
Ego complains.	Spirit transforms.
Ego demands.	Spirit participates.
Ego blames.	Spirit forgives.
Ego is confused.	Spirit is clear.
Ego protects.	Spirit knows no harm.
Ego resists.	Spirit is willing.
Ego holds its position.	Spirit looks again.

Ask your ego to join you in letting Spirit lead the way in your life.

Challenges and Difficulties

Challenges come for many reasons.

All of them can be used for Good.

Difficulties come from different causes.

All of them can be used for Good.

Conflicts occur with diverse beliefs.

All of them can be used for Good.

Disasters may happen from a multitude of causes.

All of them can be used for Good.

Humanity is resilient with forgiveness

and suffers with resistance.

Humanity regenerates with hope

and destroys itself with bitterness.

Humanity overcomes with faith

and is defeated with distrust.

Each of us has a part to play

as we look to each new day.

What will you choose ?   Forgiveness or suffering?

What are you giving ? Hope or skepticism**?**

How are you living ? With faith or uncertainty?

We are teaching our world with every thought, every word and every deed!

Stating the Obvious!

If you want to be happy, act like it!

If you want to make friends, be friendly.

If you want life to be easy, choose the easy path.

If you want to enjoy your life, seek out the Joy.

If you want to feel positive, be grateful for all the good.

If you want to grow, challenge yourself.

If you want to be different, think differently from your peers.

If you want to not suffer, leave painful situations.

If you want to be forgiving, stop judging yourself and others.

If you want to clear guilt, forgive yourself of everything.

If you want to be unafraid, trust in a Higher Power.

If you want to be healthy, think, talk and act healthy.

If you want to live simply, let go of clutter and complexity.

If you want to be honest, tell the truth.

If you want to be prosperous, appreciate your resources.

If you want to be loving, give your love unconditionally.

If you want to be beautiful, see and enjoy your beauty.

If you want to help someone, give them what will be helpful.

If you want to be free, let go of everything that limits you.

If you want to succeed, acknowledge your successes.

If you want to be confident, trust yourself.

If you want to be in love, love yourSelf and your life!

If you want to feel fulfilled, give yourSelf what you really want.

If you want to be connected with Spirit, tune in.

Keep Your Agreements

To build self esteem, confidence and trust in Yourself,

KEEP YOUR AGREEMENTS!

And if you have not kept agreements and broken promises, **FORGIVE YOURSELF!**

Many times people find it difficult to trust others and easy to doubt themselves. Our doubts and skepticism are due to our own lack of loyalty, impeccability and follow-through.

It is as simple as telling your children you will be there "in a minute", but take an hour. Or start a diet and then quit the next day. Or make an appointment for ten o'clock, but arrive 20 minutes late. Or vow, "for richer, for poorer, in sickness and in health, to love and to cherish" and then divorce. Or agree to pay your bills on time, but are late. Or promise to work for what you earn, but take more breaks to talk and eat and email than are allowed.

What promises have you been forgetting? What agreements do you break? How much do you trust yourself and others? How confident are you in your relationships? Are you willing to forgive and make the changes needed?

Agreements are the fabric of relationships.

They bring us together and hold us in trust.

Our freedom is in changing our agreements overtly with the awareness of both parties beforehand (not after the fact). When a promise is made, we honor the sacred trust of our relationship. Our follow-through is the demonstration of our value for ourselves and the other. When we consciously choose to quit on an agreement made, we imply "You are not important in my life." And we teach ourselves, we are not to be trusted.

Rather than go along with what others are doing or have done to us, we must stand for honorable principles and respectful relationships. By making and keeping agreements, we build integrity and trust in ourselves. We teach commitment and responsibility to others. We learn to trust in a world where we are responsible for our own behavior, not others' behavior. Until our agreements are kept, we cannot expect others to believe us or trust us or learn from us.

So let us forgive our errors and choose again. Make and keep your promises. Learn to trust in your own worth by keeping your agreements with yourself and your loved ones. Be honest and honorable. Be willing to say, "I am sorry." Choose again for the Highest Good for all concerned. Be confident in your choices and agreements. Believe in Yourself. Start with small do-able agreements, so you don't let yourself down. Under-commit to begin to change.

How Do You Know You Are Loved?

I am awake and inspired, free to choose with nothing to lose.

I have a sense of electricity, blissful ecstasy.

I know I Am Me!

There is forgiveness and release in my mind.

There is joy and gratitude in my heart.

There is vision and creativity in my Spirit.

I can see everything clearly and Love everyone dearly.

Life works without any effort for I have realized what really IS.

I am never lonely for there is inner Union with All.

I am never lost for there is an inner Light to guide my way.

I am never lacking for there is trust in the Abundance I AM.

I am never doubtful, for the certainty of "All is Well" is my Truth.

I LOVE LIFE AND LIFE LOVES ME.

ONLY LOVE DO I SEE

AND IT FILLS ME WITH GLEE.

SO WHAT ELSE COULD I BE?

I AM LOVING YOU AS YOU REMEMBER LOVE.

LOVE

Whatever you do, Do it with LOVE!

Whenever you give, Give with LOVE!

Wherever you are, Be there with LOVE!

However you choose, Choose with LOVE!

LOVE is the Answer!

LOVE is the Guide!

LOVE is the Reason for Every Season!

There is no one better to LOVE than the One you are with!

There is no better reason to LOVE than simply "because"!

There is no better goal to achieve than to LOVE every ONE!

There is no better outcome than to experience more LOVE!

You are the LOVE Bringer.

You are LOVE'S key.

You are LOVE'S answer.

Only LOVE will you see.

Happy days are here again,

When you always let LOVE win!

There is no mistake You ever make, except when you forget to LOVE. Then excuse your mistake, as you quickly take the steps to remember to LOVE!

Interconnected

What if there really is only One of us, One Son or Creation of God? What if we are like cells or individual parts in the whole body of humanity? What if all parts of the body of humanity were created to work together, as do the cells and organs in our individual physical bodies? What if when a part malfunctions or forgets to participate and contribute, it is up to the other parts that notice to communicate, to fill in, to wake up the forgetful part? What if working together we experience total wholeness, goodness and abundance?

What if when we take over and compensate for a missing part, we throw the whole body off balance? What if participating parts of the whole are called to show up, pay attention and tell the truth? What if there really is only wholeness and the call to remember wholeness?

If you are a part of me, then I would give to you according to how I give to myself in that way. If we are One, then I will wake you up to play and participate with me fully consciously. If some parts want to forget and die to their current state of being, those parts will be replaced. We can jumpstart one another with our natural expressions of truth.

We are our brother's keeper. We are all interrelated. Each one's lack and limitation is ours. We are the same, you and I. We are all in this together.

Circle of Influence

In your wholeness, I am healed.

In your blessing, I am blessed.

In your abundance, I have plenty.

In your happiness, I surely rejoice.

There is every reason to celebrate you and our lives joined in Holy Reunion. We are forever a gift of loving reminders for one another.

Make this day of giving thanks one in which you receive my appreciation for your conscious living and your abundant giving. Each of us has a circle of influence, a community, a family in which we live and share and care. This is your place to be the initiator, the teacher and leader and healer, the person of principle and authentic sharing that you are.

As you give, you build a world of givers.

As you remember your reason for being, you awaken others to their unique purpose.

As you share yourSelf and your Love, you teach others to reach out with Love.

And as you live your life with abundant joy and good will, you inspire your world to do the same.

We are in this world together, you and I.

And together, we make a big difference!

I Forgive

If everything and everyone in my life is a reflection of my consciousness (the conscious and unconscious thoughts, pictures, visions, beliefs, programs, rules, and agreements which I hold in my mind/computer), then I choose to forgive myself for every place where I am not clear, whole, godly, beautiful, and joyful.

I forgive any moment where I have not been conscious and thoughtful.

I forgive any act of ignorance, selfishness, demand, or fear.

I forgive any preaching or teaching which implied, "Do it my way."

I forgive any relationship based on need or greed.

I forgive any choice made from duty or obligation.

I forgive any gift given from expectation or pacification.

I forgive any emotional displays which created guilt or separation.

I forgive any loss or lack or littleness which taught falsely.

I forgive any helpfulness that led to dependency or self-criticism.

I forgive any and all activities which were not used to serve the Good of All Beings.

I forgive any unconscious acts of omission or commission which did not serve Good.

I forgive myself for any time I have been hurt, offended, defended, guilty or frightened.

I forgive myself for forgetting I Am Love and I am loving.

I forgive myself for stepping away from or avoiding difficult situations.

I forgive myself for getting sick.

I forgive myself for blaming anyone for my experience.

I am willing to grant all these same forgivenesses to everyone everywhere.

I trust with true and wholehearted forgiveness all things are made whole.

I know the miracle of love will heal all things.

I trust in my little willingness to learn to love more purely day by day.

I believe in the true healing power of forgiveness.

Your Best Self

If you would grow to your best self,

Be patient, not demanding

Accepting, not condemning

Nurturing, not withholding

Self-marveling, not belittling

Gently guiding, not pushing & punishing.

For you are more sensitive than you know.

Mankind is tough as war

Yet delicate as flowers.

We can endure agonies

But we open fully only to warmth & light.

And our need to grow

Is fragile as a fragrance

Dispersed by storms of will

To return only when those storms are still

So accept, respect,

Attend your sensitivity.

A flower cannot be opened with a hammer

Anonymous

Love No Matter What

Only Love is Real, Everything else is illusion.

Life is about sorting out the illusion from the Truth.

"Where is the Love in this and every situation?"

This is our spiritual sorting mechanism.

When in doubt, let go of your position and simply LOVE.

When in conflict, let go of your confusion and choose to LOVE.

When in fear, let go of your judgments and remember LOVE.

When in separation, let go of your comparison and LOVE the other.

When in grief, let go of your sorrow and Love through the veil of death.

When in guilt, let go of your blame, forgive your mistakes and LOVE yourSelf.

When lost in the illusion, let go of your attachments and LOVE God.

The only mistake we ever make is when we forget to LOVE.

I am willing to Love no matter what.

In Faith

Forgiveness is faith made manifest.

In faith I release the past.
In faith I trust in the future.
In faith I cease defending.
In faith I reach out with love.
In faith I give All to All.
In faith I speak my Truth.
In faith I see the Goodness all around me.
In faith I serve God and the Highest Good I know.
In faith I listen within and follow.
In faith I heal my mind and my body.
In faith I remember the Peace of God.
In faith I know All is well.
In faith I live united with my Creator.

Forgive all doubt and uncertainty.
Forgive lack and limitation.
Forgive judgment and separation.
Forgive fear and harm.
Forgive all that is not of God and Goodness.

Our Faith leads us to Forgive.

Detachment

Letting go allows going with the flow. Going with the flow requires letting go. Such is the natural cycle of life. Everything changing and ever the same.

Allowing ourselves to release that which is not essential, brings freedom and simplicity. Being with and blessing what is now, opens the heart to fulfillment and inner trust. In fully receiving the gifts of today, we have no anxiety about tomorrow. Today is the first day and the only day to fully enjoy the present goodness and beauty. When we maximize the peace and love and joy today, tomorrow takes care of itself.

Breathe in the bountiful blessings. Savor every moment.

Give joy-filled thanks. And let it all go.

Receive the next beautiful blessing with wonder and delight. Be as a child. And inherit the earth.

The changing life cycle moves us through a natural learning and growing process as we expand our willingness to freely give and receive. There is infinite goodness and abundance here for us.

It is our choice as to when we wholly receive All That Is given. Life is fun, safe and easy when we let go.

Love is an action of detachment, release and freedom. So love is letting go!

Tired of Being Tired?

What creates fatigue:
1. Fear and worry
2. Judgment and self-criticism
3. Trying too hard.
4. Figuring out all the details
5. Trying to never make a mistake
6. Getting stuck where you are
7. Being in conflict. (I want to, but I can't)
8. Seeking external approval
9. Following others' advice
10. Getting distracted by demands & distraction
11. Unhealed pain and unsolved problems
12. Shame and guilt
13. Disappointment and depression
14. Pretending to be something you are not
15. Resisting resistance
16. Waiting for someone or something.
17. Disrespecting your Self
18. Spiritual confusion, not knowing your values

Living on Purpose

"What makes the difference between happy, successful, fulfilling lives and non-productive, half-hearted, depressing and anxious lives?

How can we live lives that really work vs. lives full of complaining, misery, poor health, and minimal satisfaction?

1. Focus on your highest values.
2. Be clear about the life you want.
3. State your conscious intention to succeed.
4. Apply and practice what you have learned.
5. Make the details as important as your overall goals.
6. Persevere until you accomplish.
7. Improve constantly and immediately change what isn't working to support your values and goals.
8. Appreciate yourself and your work for success.

Love Is The Answer

It's never too late to say, "I'm sorry."
It's never too late to make amends.
It's never too late to be forgiving.
It's never too late to help old friends.

It's never too late to say, "I love you."
It's never too late to serve them now.
It's never too late to have the courage
To give my help and a sacred vow.

Now is the moment which I have.
This is the time which I can give
All of my love and my lasting commitment
Love is the answer and the way I live.

It is never too late!
Forgive and live!
Choose again right now!

Time For Action

Enough talking!

Enough wishing!

Enough reading!

Enough hoping!

Enough sitting!

Enough waiting!

It is time! Move into doing something to change your life.

Get off the couch. Get out of bed. Get up from the table!

Clean out the cupboards. Organize your refrigerator.

Eat right. Be conscious and grateful.

Prepare nutritional meals with gratitude and consciousness.

Clean your house with gratitude and consciousness.

Empty your garbage with gratitude and consciousness.

Talk to your family with gratitude and consciousness.

Get ready for your day with gratitude and consciousness.

Plan your week with gratitude and consciousness.

Let go of all you don't utilize with gratitude and consciousness.

Utilize your resources (time, energy and money) with gratitude and consciousness.

How you live is a statement of who you are.

Real Relationships

Do you hunger for intimacy, closeness, friendship, belonging, being really valued?

Authentic relationships are intimate, connected, equal, respectful, appreciative, genuine, meaningful and right-intentioned.

To begin to discover and create these relationships, we must first begin with ourselves.

Take time to get acquainted with yourself. Alone time with a journal. Ask yourself meaningful questions as you would want to know from a real friend. For example: "What matters most to me?" "How do I want to live my life day by day?" "What do I value most in a friend?"

Then, do what matters.

Live like today is your last and be the friend you value.

The Law of Attraction will bring to you those with whom you can best heal and grow.

Judgment Gets You Stuck

The experience of life goes into slow motion or pause as you doubt and distrust, to examine, evaluate and criticize what is happening. To breathe, to release to Spirit, to forgive, to trust, to be willing, and to let go, opens the flow to see the gift of what is, to appreciate, and to move us on into the next moment.

Literally, judgment and criticism (both positive and negative) cause the mind to stop and search the scene for confirming evidence. We seek for experiences to support our beliefs, attitudes and thoughts. FEAR= false evidence and experiences appearing real.

Choose to appreciate

    and life moves us into the next appreciation.

Choose to denigrate ourselves

    and we seek more self-criticism.

Choose to worry

    and there is more to be of concern.

Choose to bless everyone and everything,

    and our lives seem totally blessed.

Choose to try to understand and figure out a person

    and it becomes more complicated.

The path we take yields the experience we make for ourselves.

The Truth about Real Relationships

Every encounter is holy.

1. All relationships are equally important. No one greater or lesser, more or less special.

2. Every relationship is practice and refinement for every other relationship.

3. Everyone is our teacher and gives us opportunities to heal as we teach and learn with one another.

4. Everyone is a mirror. How we perceive another is how we judge ourselves. How we treat another is how we learn to treat ourselves. What we see is our opportunity to condemn or forgive.

5. We are as much responsible for what we receive as for what we give. What you expect (feel you deserve) is what you get. We are teaching others what and how to give to us with our thoughts, words and deeds.

6. All relationship problems are issues of separation and fear of authority.

7. All relationship solutions are willingness to forgive, to choose again, to extend love, to trust and forgive.

Are You Ready?

Are you willing to have a new beginning, to co-create a new world?

Are you open to play your part fully and freely giving your gifts?

What is the world you want?

Get a clear picture and describe it all!

Then begin with yourself, your attitudes, habits and behaviors.

Act as you want others in your world to live and give.

Teach by your example.

Release the past with your forgiveness.

Respond to fearfulness with Love.

Wakeup the forgetful by remembering.

Give the eternal lasting stuff to the empty.

Show others how to stay in love.

The One Who Knows is called to teach.

The One Who Remembers is called to remind.

The One Who Loves is called to reach out.

The One Who is Abundant is called to share.

The One Who is Free is called to set free.

We are all in this together—here to give and receive, teach and learn. All of us are waking up to be respectful and responsible in our cooperative co-creation!

Freedom

Freedom to live in your chosen style?
Freedom to speak your own truth?
Freedom to relate with those whom you trust?
Freedom to create with sings to your heart?

We are free to eat what and where and when we want.
We are free to watch what and how much we choose.
We are free to work or not work at whatever job we wish.
We are free to study and learn whatever interests us.
We are free to speak or not speak about any topic under the sun.
We are free to value or not value anything we choose.
We are free to travel and visit anywhere in the world.
We are free to believe and worship anything we wish.
We are free to feel anyway we want: happy, sad, peaceful or mad.

We really are free beings.
Let us be grateful for the infinite freedom we have.
Let us take full responsibility for the choices we make.
Let us truly respect the freedoms we share.

Love is Freedom and Trust

When I live freely trusting, I experience Joy.

My life is about living and giving this message:

I am free.

I am trusting.

Therefore I am filled with Joy.

What is your life's message?

What is your Truth?

How do you live and give your message?

Loving you and me.

Trusting you and me.

Freeing you and me.

And being so joyful to see

All We are created to be.

Keep Your Life On Track

This is my simplest and most basic answer.

1) Sit alone and simply listen to your inner Voice, the essential You, 5-15 min. Daily. (No distractions, music, interruptions, making lists or plans. Just listen in silence.)

2) Ingest the best and forget the rest. Associate with the most enlightened and successfully loving people. Drink an abundance of pure water. Eat only healthy life-giving foods. Breathe fresh air. Spend time enjoying nature.

3) Keep your promises and commitments to yourself. Act step by step and persevere until you have reached your self-made goals. Know where you are going and keep on going until you get there.

4) Think, act and speak with confidence and courage. Both language and physiology all affect our attitude. "I am.....,

   I can...., I must........, I choose........."

Live as if you were a conscious, committed, confident purposeful and successful person!

It is amazing how quickly you will notice that you are!

How fun, safe, and easy to Be All You Can Be!

Created to Create

If your life is as a Creative Instrument of God's Infinite Love and Creative Power, where do you begin?

Begin by receiving the Gift.

I am an Instrument of the Divine.

I have within me God's Creative Power.

Practice what you have been given.

I am open to the guidance of my Inner Teacher.

I am willing to express my creative potential.

Appreciate your willingness and your gift.

I thank my Creator for the miracles of Creation in my life.

I fully enjoy and appreciate my life of creative loving and learning.

Claim your inheritance with purpose, and prayer.

I am here to create what is good and beautiful and holy.

I joyfully choose to allow the creative potential within me to be freely expressed.

Trust your Source, your Self and your Gifts.

I trust in the Power and "Presents" of God within me.

I am an extension of God's Love and Light here and now.

You are All that You claim to be and more.

Golden Rule

Do unto others as You would have them do unto You.

Give to another what you would want to receive in the same circumstance. All that You give is given to YourSelf.

The more you love and respect yourSelf, the more You love and respect others.

The more you love and respect yourSelf, the more others love and respect you.

The more you love and respect yourSelf, the more others love and respect themselves.

What goes around, comes around.

You reap what you have sown.

What you see in another is the perception and interpretation that you have laid upon yourself.

To the degree you forgive yourself, you will love and forgive others.

What you perceive in another, you strengthen in yourself.

The healing of God's creation (children) is all the world is for.

It is our function to erase the mistakes of humanity and choose again for Goodness and Mercy.

As we judge a brother, we judge ourselves and fear the judgment of others.

Through forgiveness, we open to a new moment and a new possibility where we can see the Light within.

Giving

What is it about **"giving"** that frightens the ego, the personality, the human self?

To the ego:

To give is to Lose. To get is to win.

To win at life is to give as little as possible and to get or gain as much as possible.

To Spirit:

To give is to win. To get or take is meaningless.

To win at life: Give All to All to Have All.

What we invest in, we experience as important in our lives.

When we invest in **acquiring more**, ego never experiences enough.

When we invest in **giving More,** Spirit always has enough to give.

Ego gives away what it has acquired, and believes it has lost.

Spirit shares All that it has, and experiences expanded fulfillment.

Life is for giving. You are the Gift.

It is in giving that you recognize the gift You Are and the gifts you have!

All that you give is really and truly given to your Whole Self.

Everything we give to One is given to All.

Everything we deny even One, we deny All.

To Heal MySelf

I now choose to love myself in every way, every day.

To love myself, I make Love-based choices.

I forgive myself for being afraid.

To heal myself is to be happy and live in Love.

To stay healthy is to cease using my body lovelessly.

All sickness and disease is a wakeup call, an invitation to choose again, to find a better way.

Illness and disease have been unconsciously chosen to give me something I think I want.

I can choose to get attention or the rest I need without getting sick.

I can always forgive my choices and choose again for a better way to meet my spiritual and emotional needs..

I am responsible for how I use every experience.

I now use everything as an opportunity to wake up.

I choose to remember the Truth no matter what the apparency.

I am whole and happy and free.

I am as God created me.

I know I am Whole and Good and Beautiful!

I respect my Whole and Holy Self.

I choose healing partners who see me as Whole.

I know I am healed.

Peace Must Come First!

For total health, there must be peace.

For real happiness, there must be peace.

For self-confidence, there must be peace.

For perfect trust, there must be peace.

For complete understanding, there must be peace.

For family harmony, there must be peace.

For conscious decisions, there must be peace.

For absolute freedom, there must be peace.

For ease and flow, there must be peace.

For Spiritual connection, there must be peace.

For abundant living, there must be peace.

For joyful giving, there must be peace.

For unity and cooperation, there must be peace.

For spiritual healing, there must be peace.

Forgive everyone and everything all the time.
Forgive yourSelf.
Then Peace will be in your Mind and experiences.
Forgive with every breath.

Peace be with You.

Beliefs

Some have walked away from traditional religion and have chosen a path of personal spirituality. Some have chosen to "translate" the words of past religion into a more universal understanding. And some have totally abandoned believing in anything greater than themselves.

Your life demonstrates what you believe. How you live tells volumes about your values.

Your testimony is in what you say and do .

So what do you believe? In good? In love? In light? In hope? In possibilities? In bad? In fear? In darkness? In limitations?

What you believe shines through your life in how you live.

And who and what is your "God"? Health? Money? The Great Unknown? Being your Best Self?

Your area of focus on becomes your guiding light.

How are you choosing to live? Giving or getting as much as you can? Pushing or holding back on your hopes and dreams? Waiting or willing for Good to appear in your life? Accepting or resisting the experiences you have? Trusting or fearing what each day brings?

You can choose a philosophy which honors the Good, encourages trust, is willing to act, gives freely of Love, learns from each encounter, and knows fulfillment as the outcome.

What I Believe

What I believe is obvious.

You read my beliefs.

You hear my words.

You see my activities.

Everywhere and all the time, I am living what I believe.

I believe in open honest expression.

I believe in total freedom of thought.

I believe in the intrinsic inherent Good.

I believe in being happy and healthy.

I believe in miracles of hope and faith.

I believe in living fully and abundantly.

I believe in learning and loving and letting go.

I believe in possibilities, options and choices.

I believe in you and me and all of us together.

What do you believe?

Are you living what you believe?

Integrity makes life fun, safe, and easy.

Live what you believe.

Consciousness

How can you tell a conscious Being?

They create for themselves:
- a clean house
- a pure diet
- conscious relationships
- a beautiful environment
- an orderly life
- a respect for nature
- a love for Self
- total forgiveness
- a fulfilling work
- learning from everything
- grateful attitude
- cooperation with all creatures
- taking full responsibility for their experience

Be conscious and conscientious.

Be Here Now

Show up!

Pay attention!

Tell the Truth!

Detach from the Outcome!

Usually every morning early, I sit down at the keyboard.

    I show up!

I breathe easily. My mind is alert and open and willing!

    I pay attention!

I allow the ideas, concepts and words to flow without scrutiny!

    I tell the truth!

I am complete and let go of any need for anything more.

    I detach from the outcome!

This is the key to a life of effortless flow, seeking nothing and expecting the Highest Good for All concerned. I of myself can do nothing, but Spirit within me works gently through me. I am grateful to be a willing participant in this natural flow of creativity and healing for myself and those who walk with me.

I trust that whatever message I receive is always for Me. And perhaps some or all of the messages that are written are for You as well.

May our journey together be a blessing for Us All!

Introvert or Extrovert?

In our Western culture, we tend to exalt the **extrovert**.

In the Eastern culture the **introvert** is exalted.

Let's look at what you are to give yourself permission to be.

Extraverts prefer drawing energy from the outside world of people, activities or things. **Introverts** prefer drawing energy from one's inner world of ideas, emotions or visions.

Extraverts communicate energy and enthusiasm, respond quickly and spontaneously, focus on people and things in external environment, enjoy communicating in groups, prefer face to face over written, and like talking out loud to come to conclusions. **Introverts** keep energy and enthusiasm inside, like to think before responding, focus on inner ideas and thoughts, need to be drawn out, prefer one-to one- and written communication and verbalize already well thought out conclusions.

Extroverts prefer variety and action in work situations, are often impatient with long slow jobs, are interested in the activities of their work and how others do it. They often act quickly, develop ideas though discussion and enjoy having others around. **Introverts** like quiet for concentration, tend to like working on a project for a long time without

interruption, are interested in the ideas behind their work, like to think a lot before acting, may find phone calls intrusive, develop ideas by reflection, and like working alone.

Are you honoring your uniqueness?

Be Unique! Be You!

All of us are different.

All of us are unique.

Some prefer to listen.

Some prefer to speak.

Each one of us plays our part.

The way we're called to do.

Each one of us displays our Heart.

To our Self we must be true.

Listen to what your heart confides

When you still and quiet your mind.

Follow the spark of joy inside.

True happiness will you find.

Life is our learning classroom.

And Love will light the way.

As we learn the lessons of integrity

Being true to our Inner Voice all day.

You already know what matters to you.

You know the Joy you feel.

Act on your principles and priorities.

And you will live a life that is Real!

All Are Chosen

I open to inspiration within, the Inner Guidance, the Highest Good, the Joy that moves through me like the wind in the trees. And then I share freely what my heart calls me to express spontaneously with all the love I Am. I am always loving you with words and activities and with being the Love and seeing the Love we are.

Writing and sharing these loving reminders are first received by my Self as gift and blessing, sometimes a Holy Lesson, with joyous appreciation. They are my opportunity to connect in a sacred and intimate way to the inner calling of my Spirit. Thanks to a spiritual teacher who spoke simply to me in 1976, "Why not **sit for five minutes a day and do nothing**?" I did and it changed my life.

For in this simple process I found instantly I could see and hear spiritual vision and guidance. It was a great natural joy which I valued and have done daily every since. Sometimes philosophical, sometimes answers to questions, sometimes clear direction, sometimes healing and clearing limiting thinking and misperceptions, sometimes just loving me and reminding me who I AM.

I am eternally grateful to have received this gift and share it with you. I am reminding you that this gift is available for all who are open. There are no special gifts for the chosen ones.

All are chosen.

All are given spiritual gifts.

To love unconditionally is to receive the infinite gifts of Spirit.

Polish Your Diamond

When you polish your whole life, like a stone, to the brilliance of a diamond, don't be surprised, if those around you don't recognize you for who you are.

Remember, we can only see others to the degree to which we can see ourselves!

When we see someone shining brightly, as we wish we would,

We may feel jealous, angry, even guilty and ashamed,

because we haven't done the work to polish our own lives.

Often we wish we could be beautiful, holy and good,

but still carry the beliefs and attitudes and activities

which keep our intrinsic worth hidden from our view.

Don't allow others judgments, envy, even anger

to create Self-doubt or Self-diminishment.

Be freely All that You Are.

Shine brightly.

Give freely.

Share your joy.

Let others learn from their own lack of Self Love

to choose again to fully be the beautiful shining light.

When we learn to free, we can all be

the Beauty, Goodness and Wholeness we truly are.

Thoughts Create

Your thoughts and your words create your experience.
So be aware to use them consciously, not carelessly.

To be happy, think and speak and act happy.
To be successful, believe and behave like a successful person.
To be prosperous, give thanks for the riches you now have.
To be healthy, respect your natural health with your activities.

To curse or condemn is to create more of what you hate.
To worry and fear is to create more to be concerned about.
To feel disappointed is to seek and find more loss and lack.
To doubt and distrust yourself and your world is to generate more uncertainty.

Wherever we focus our attention, our thoughts and words and activities, we strengthen the results of our focus.

Choose to erase, forgive, and release the negative or limiting focus of the fearful and limiting mind.

Open to the expansive, creative, trusting, and joyful Mind to focus on the unlimited possibilities that await you when you transfer your allegiance from fear to faith, from worry to trust.

Changing your mind changes your life.

Affirmations

Thoughts create. What we think creates what we experience. Changing our minds changes our lives.

Therefore, clearing our minds of negative or limited thinking clears our lives. Inner healing creates outer wholeness, goodness and beauty.

I recommend using affirmations daily.

Written and spoken 20 times a day, early morning or before bedtime is best. Listening to and writing down your mind chatter (mental resistance) is valuable. An open mind filled with light and peace is the goal. With an open mind, you can let Love lead the Way and let Spirit be your guide. With a programmed mind, you will let limiting beliefs and unconscious habits lead. Affirmations are a way of cleansing or undoing the unconscious programming.

My favorites are:

I forgive myself for limiting myself.

My mind automatically erases everything that is not wholly true and wholly loving.

Everything always works more exquisitely than I can plan.

I trust, respect and support myself; therefore I am trusted, respected and supported by others.

Give yourself 30 days to experiment with 2 or 3 affirmations. Notice the changes in your life. It's worth the work!

Prayer

Prayer is the natural expression of our Holiness.

Prayer is remembering what has been forgotten.

Prayer is the longing of our minds to return to Peace.

Prayer is the gift of willingness to see all things new again.

Prayer is awakening to see the Love from which we came.

What is prayer but a call to reconnect and listen within!

What is prayer but a song of gratitude and praise!

What is prayer but the sweet memory of returning home!

What is prayer but the earnest desire that All be Well!

Prayers are the songs we sing, the tears we shed, the smiles we share.

Prayers are our affirmations of Love, our desires for success, our words of Truth.

Prayers are our words like "please" and "thanks", "hello" and "good-bye".

Prayers are our gifts, our helpfulness, our sincerity, our praise, and our loving touch.

Prayers are silent and verbal, written and demonstrated.

Prayers are remembering our natural state of Wholeness, Goodness and Beauty.

Prayers are blessings given and blessings received.

Prayers are the conscious willingness

to remember what is forever True.

"Prayer For A Loved One"

I will not worry, fret or be unhappy over you.

I will not be afraid for you.

I will not give up on you.

I will not blame, criticize or condemn you.

I will remember first, last and always that you are God's child, that you have His Spirit in you.

I will trust Spirit to take care of you,

    to be a light to your path, to provide for your needs.

I will think of you as always being surrounded by God's loving Presence, enfolded in His protecting care, as kept safe and secure in Him.

I will be patient with you.

I will stand by you in faith, and bless you in my prayers, knowing that you are growing, knowing that you are finding the help you need, the love you need, the healing you need, the financial freedom you need.

I have only good feelings in my heart about you.

I am willing to let you live your life as you see fit.

Your way may not be my way,

    but I will trust the Spirit of God in you

        to show you the way of your highest Good.

God loves you and I love you!

I have confidence in you and I believe in you!!

               (author unknown)

Your Mind is a Like a Television

You have many built in channels and you can always add more. Whether through a cable to an archived system of choices or from a satellite to more global mass consciousness, you can tune into what you choose to ponder and picture.

You can spend your mental energy watching the news, the weather, human interest stories, historical movies, tragedies and dramas, cartoons, comedy hour, MTV, cultural entertainment, the buying channels, how to improve your home, etc.—all in your own mind. You can spend your time watching other peoples' lives with envy, humor, disdain or appreciation. You can focus on what is good in life or what is terrible. You can be entertained, terrorized, inspired or bored with the current selection of thought patterns or mental TV. You are at choice.

Likewise you can broadcast in much the same way, simply by adding your thoughts to the world around you. What you focus on, you attract into your world. What you pay attention to, you increase. What you sow with your consciousness, you reap in your experience. What you think about, you become. "And all these things shall be added unto you". Where you place the attention in your mind, you will yield the conceived outcome. What we think and say and do is teaching our world, even unconsciously..

Your mind is both a receiver and broadcaster of whatever you choose to tune into.

So what do you choose to use your mind to attract?

What do you want to receive with your mental focus?

What do you want to telecast with your mind?

What is the world you want to strengthen?

What do you want your thoughts to harvest?

You choose.

If your mind has been left to run with no guidance and structure, like an errant child, it needs training and practice. It requires time, patience, consistency and constant supervision to learn to function in a helpful and focused way. Spend time daily to teach your mind to think in ways which improve the quality of your life and the lives of others.

Your mind deserves to be watched and enjoyed only when playing the programs you want to experience in your life.

You have the controls.

Change the channel when you want a better program in life.

Life and death!

Is there life after death?
Is there death?
So what is life?

Can we know what is real?
Can we trust what we feel?
Can we ask for the best?
So we wait for the rest?

All of us are exploring these questions or avoiding them.

I have always known that these bodies are temporary costumes for our current play!

The performance for our lifetime may take on varied roles or be an ongoing part.

We take our bows, receive applause, go unnoticed, sing in the chorus, work behind the scenes, close the curtain, or simply critique others around us.

We all have chosen our place and can choose again at any time. Tragedy or comedy!

Work is steady unless we want a sabbatical, or take sick leave.

The pay varies according to our choice of parts.

And when we are done, we take off our costumes and go home.

Enjoy your life. Live life so you will have no regrets.

Saying "Good-Bye"

Truly saying "good-bye" will leave no regrets.

Often when there is an apparent ending or closure in death, divorce, transfer, moving on, there seems to be regret, sadness, grief, or resentment. When looked at deeply, there are often incompletions, old disappointments, unexpressed communication, unfulfilled dreams and promises, lack of forgiveness, both conscious and unconscious.

Consider saying, "Good-Bye." "God be with You."
"May goodness and mercy be with you now and forever."

To truly wish someone well in their journey of life changes is to release them to their Highest Good. We know not what is in the best interest of another. So it is in our best interest to let them go with love rather than asking them to wait for our sake or to judge their choices.

To **complete** our relationships is to clear up all past incompletions with communication, prayer, forgiveness and making amends. **I know I am complete when in the present moment I can easily and wholeheartedly say, "I love You." When I am not complete, I have inner work to do.**

Saying, "Good Bye" opens the door to the next "Hello".
Love never ends. It only changes form.

Giving Thanks

Thank those who wake you up with unloving reminders.

Thank those who wake you up with criticism and complaints.

Thank those who push your buttons.

Thank those who irritate and frustrate you.

Thank those who demand your unwanted attention.

Thank those who ask for what you resist giving.

Thank those who challenge you.

Thank those who ask questions you cannot answer.

Thank those who confuse and cloud your thinking.

Thank those who are exactly opposite what you want to be.

Everyone is our teacher.

"Remember to Love" is always the message.

HOPE: Happiness Overcomes Past Experiences.

When faced with apparent trials and tribulations, tragedies and traumas, we often lose hope. The future seems dim. There appears to be nothing to hang on to, no one to guide us, and even no reason to go on. Hope is lost. Whether a time of questioning, "dark night of the soul", depression, anger with God, or just feeling disheartened, **this is a spiritual call.**

Worldly comfort often leads to complacency, just as confusion may lead us to Spiritual seeking. And where we are looking we will find what we are looking for.

When in the dark, look for the light.

When in doubt, seek for what is certain.

When feeling loss, look for what is lasting.

When in despair, look where there is hope.

When you are depressed, invite what is expressive.

When you are confused, seek out what is clear.

When you are in fear, look at what you love.

And when you have forsaken God, has God forsaken you?

The questioner will find the answers.

The hopeless find miracles exist.

The grieved will learn life goes on.

And the alone recognizes we are All One.

Release what you no longer want. Seek what is missing.

Conscious prayerful requests are fulfilled.

Charity and Contribution

Faith, Hope and Charity—all three are expressions of your Love for Self, Source and others.

To give with an open heart and mind is to give to oneself. There is no pity, no fixing, no feeling sorry for, no self-aggrandizement, no need to receive, no need to be acknowledged. Giving is our natural state as we recognize, express and extend the Love we are.

To give to ourselves and to others is simply a "loving reminder" that Love is always and in all ways present. Charity and contribution are giving tribute to that Loving Presence in every One at all times. When another has forgotten, feels needy or lacking, receiving your Love will prime their Love pump, and open the possibility of seeking the wellspring of Love within. Often a healing for someone who feels needy is to have them give to another in order to reawaken the abundance of Love within themselves.

Consider giving today for the purpose of reminding rather than making up for what another seems to have lost or be lacking.

Give today to remind yourself.

Give today to inspire your world with the truth.

Give today to shine where light may be dim.

Give today to celebrate the Love you are.

How Do You Like to Be Loved?

We each have our favorite ways of expressing our love. And we have our most touching ways of knowing we are loved by another.

Gifts are a gesture of Love.

For some, flowers, dinner out, a special gift or trip are the ideal way to give and receive love.

Affection is an act of Love.

For some, physical touch, hugs, holding hands, sexual intimacy, a back rub are the best.

Quality time is a demonstration of Love.

Taking time to sit and listen, to walk and talk together, to share deeply is the most meaningful for some.

Affirming words are an expression of Love.

For some positive words, written and spoken, are the truest form of love expressed.

Acts of service are Love made tangible.

For some being helpful, working side by side, performing a thoughtful act is most believable.

To give to another what you want in return may be confusing. Ask your friends and family how they would most feel loved by you. Then let them know your favorite way of being loved.

30 Days to Enlightenment and Freedom

Begin now to free yourSelf, and awaken to Who You really Are!

Every morning,

Write 30 Forgivenesses. i.e. "I forgive…. I forgive…….

I forgive….."etc. Forgive whatever comes to mind.

Then spend 2-5 minutes toning (chanting) "Ahhhhh".

Immediately following **write 30 Choices**. i.e. "I choose….. I choose……" Write whatever comes up.

Every evening,

Write 30 gratitudes. i.e. "I appreciate….. I am grateful for….." etc.

Then spend 2-5 minutes toning or chanting the sound "Ommmm"

Remember to keep breathing fully, freely, easily throughout.

Practice this simple, profoundly effective exercise for 30 days

 …or for the rest of your life to be free!

I dare you to quit reinvesting your time and energy and resources on lifetime patterns and unconscious habits that don't bring happiness or peace of mind.

This works! It is simple but true!

Spiritual Tips for Abundant Living

1. Honor and respect your Self.
2. Do what you love and love what you do.
3. Appreciate what you have.
4. Stop complaining, wishing and fantasizing.
5. Clarify what ego wants and what Spirit wants.
6. Recognize the difference between temporal pleasures and eternal treasures.
7. Spend less than you earn.
8. Notice that you always have more than enough to share.
9. Expect life to work for you and your happiness.
10. Spirit-guided choices never require explanation, justification or convincing.
11. Get clear on your Real priorities (health, kids, travel, service, retirement, etc.)
12. Set aside the money needed for the most important things and live on what's left.
13. Give yourSelf and others only what is useful, valuable and inspiring.
14. Be grateful you live in the wealthiest society in the world.

Living on Purpose

The way of the Tao is to allow ourselves
to be one with the natural flow of life.

The life philosophies of "Live and let live",
"Let go and let God", "Don't push the river",
and "Don't worry, be happy",
all describe living life on purpose.

There is an 'inner sense' and innocence in how
we live everyday with whatever is given us.

In the present, trust will settle every problem
and answer every question.

Life on purpose is never rushed nor slowed down.
It has its own natural rhythm and movement.
It seeks for nothing and enjoys everything.
All moments are the only moment.
It is almost as if there is no time.
We need nothing and expect nothing.
The moment offers everything.

Honor the moment.

Death and Dying

Life is letting go of fear.

Death is releasing the body.

Life is learning from physical experience.

After "Life" is learning from Being.

Energy cannot be created or destroyed.

Love never ends. It simply changes form.

We are not our body. We are free.

We are as God created us to be.

Birthing requires letting go of the comfortable womb where we get used to wearing a body.

"Dying" requires releasing a sometimes uncomfortable body and challenging physical life.

Perhaps dying is birthing into new life in a different form.

Can we help both birthing and dying be a love and faith-filled experience?

Are we willing to let go of our dread and fear and simply extend Love?

Is it possible that the mystery of life, both coming and going, are meant to be a surprise?

Can we trust enough to release our need to control the outcome and the experience?

In every moment there is dying to the old and being born again.

Keys to Conscious Creation

Awareness: Stop, look around, and listen to what is now in your life.

Acknowledgment: Be honest about what you see, hear and feel both inside and out!

Allowance: Let go and release what is no longer of value (ideas, activities, and stuff).

Aha: Be still and rest in the opennenss and freedom of the unknown.

Affirmation: Choose consciously for what is now being called forth in you.

Acceptance: Trust what you need to have and experience is yours right now.

Appreciation: Enjoy and be grateful for all you have created, released and re-created.

Basic Truths:

You are unconsciously creating what you now experience.

Your love for yourself determines what you choose in life.

Your willingness to forgive the past determines your state of consciousness.

With trust in Spirit, you let the Love within you lead the way.

You consciously choose what is good, and whole and beautiful in all areas of life.

Your focus is on the good that is present rather than seeking for what is missing.

You totally enjoy your life as you have created it to be.

Enjoy the Show

All the world is our stage. We are the actors in the play of our choosing. To the degree we are aware of the Being beneath the role and the costume, we are free, detached and enlightened. To the degree we believe, identify with or feel victimized by our act, we are caught in the illusion of the physical world.

You are more than your body.

You are more than your belongings.

You are more than your roles.

You are more than your relationships.

You are more than your creations.

You are more than your service.

It is through our body and our belongings that we learn to share and contribute.

It is through our roles and relationships that we learn to forgive and love unconditionally.

It is through creativity and service that we learn to create beauty, goodness and wholeness.

Every part that we play, we write, produce and direct to learn to fully be and express the Love We Are. Show up for rehearsals. Pay attention to your inner Director. And deliver your lines with the most Truth you know.

Sit back and enjoy how life really works.

Negative Thinking

When we have just a few doubts, conscious or unconscious, life will have a few moments of doubt. We will experience some lack of fun, safety and ease according to our beliefs. The true believer literally translates everything to fit into their belief system. When I am looking for safety, fun and ease, I will find it. When I am looking for danger, seriousness and difficulty, I will find it. Our minds scan for confirmation of our current programming or beliefs. We are like giant magnets attracting the experiences we believe we will have. When we are conflicted we will have conflicting experiences.

How do we change limiting beliefs and negative thinking?

We must erase, release and forgive the false, and affirm, embrace and encourage the True. We must delete from our computer the negative programming and confirming evidence.

We must bring to consciousness all the thoughts that have held us limited and lacking. As we affirm (say and write) again and again, the mind rebels and spits out its resistance. By continuing to affirm the True, we are deleting what is false.

My mind automatically erases everything that is not wholly true and wholly loving. When you say or think or act in a limiting or negative way, say "Delete" or "Cancel". Choose again, obviously & consciously, for what you want to think, say or do. **Cancel negative thinking. Choose to be positive.**

Seeing

We give everything we see the meaning it has for us.

By our judgments, right or wrong, good or bad, we define our world.

With our own definition, the way we perceive, we create our personal experience.

Two people can see and hear the same thing and experience it totally differently.

We can choose to see our experiences differently.

Perceptions are usually based on our past experiences and how we judged them.

With a forgiving mind we can see our past experiences healed.

With a judging mind we will re-experience our past patterns of pain.

With a light-filled mind we see the Light.

With resentment and guilt we live in the dark.

Everything is either Love being extended
    or the call for Love.

Receive the Love that is given
    to open the constant flow of Love.

Respond to the call for Love
    by extending your Love to open the flow.

Ingest the Best and Forget the Rest!

Is it best for you to read the newspaper?

Is it best for you to watch television advertising?

Is it best for you to listen to sad or negative lyrics?

Is it best for you to participate in gossip?

Is it best for you to commiserate with friends?

Is it best for you to spend time feeling sorry?

Is it best for you to drink and eat too much?

Is it best for you to spend more money than you have?

Is it best for you to suffer in silence?

Is it best for you to neglect your own needs?

Is it best for you to look on the dark side of life?

Read inspiring and hopeful news.

Watch programs that are truly entertaining.

Listen to uplifting music.

Participate in positive conversations.

Encourage, love and bless your friends.

Spend your time feeling grateful.

Drink, eat and spend in moderation.

Spend money you have on what you really want.

Acknowledge your feelings and choose what you prefer.

Remember to fill your own life with love and joy first.

Look on life with a sense of childlike delight,

appreciation and open-mindedness.

Let Go

Letting go is fun, safe and easy.

I easily and gently release everything I no longer need.

My mind automatically erases every thought that is not wholly True and wholly Loving.

The past is not here. I live and choose right now.

Everything I need is here in this moment to be used for Good.

If you love something very much, let it go. If it is meant to be yours, it will return.

Love is an action of detachment.

As we trust in the spirit of Goodness and Love, we realize we need not hold on. For in clinging, we expend much energy and distract ourselves from enjoying what we have right now. It is in truly letting go of everything that we recognize what is really ours forever.

Love is You and You are Love.

This is given.

Everything else is part of the discovery process.

As you let go, you recognize the simple Truth.

Love is all you need.

And Love is Who You Are.

When the Path Becomes Difficult

Ask yourself:

What was your original purpose in choosing this way?

Look for the goal which you were originally seeking.

Appreciate the gifts you have received along the way.

Give thanks to those in your life for supporting your choice.

Forgive yourself for any and all mistakes you have made.

Ask yourself if you still value the goal.

Get clear about the price you are paying for continuing.

Decide if the goal is worth the cost to you and your loved ones.

If you choose to continue:

Decide to be positive and affirming about your choice.

Everyday choose to wake up clearly affirming,

"This is a good day."

Every evening be grateful to those around you

 for supporting you.

Appreciate yourself for persisting in the challenge.

Look for ways to make your path easier.

Ask for help from those who are most able to be helpful.

Stop talking about how hard it is. (Your focus increases your experience.)

Reward yourself and others with thanks and loving moments.

If you decide to change your direction:

Listen inside for a goal that feels good and true for you.

Forgive yourself for being afraid to make another mistake.

Trust course corrections are a natural process in reaching our goals.

Forgive any misguidance or advice you have been given.

Believe you can achieve the goal you desire.

Imagine the total experience and lifestyle you want to have.

Appreciate all you have achieved and and learned.

Acknowledge the gift received from you previous choices.

Be totally willing to follow the happy path for you.

Stop looking behind you and move in the direction of your joy.

The light in you will guide your way, one step at a time.

Learning to Trust

Communication glitches, blackouts, computers and phone problems, mix ups in directions and verbal agreements. Usually there is a call to slow down, take some extra time and patience to work things out, be peaceful, and trust in the highest outcome eventually.

Whatever the reason or cause, what is, is what is! Therefore I don't stress myself with trying to make something happen. I simply let go and trust in the "right" outcome. For me it is like surrendering to Good, whenever it is going to happen. My faith tells me it will show up and I simply need to be patient.

This works with traffic backups. There is no payoff in anger, upset or fear. I need not be moved from my center of peace. And in my peace I seem to actually make a positive difference most of the time. (The one with the cool head always comes up with more creative solutions.)

So let go and trust.

Be peaceful and patient.

Allow the world to do its thing.

Enjoy the moment.

Row, row, row your boat

Gently down the stream.

Merrily, merrily, merrily, merrily

Life is but a dream!

What's Right?

How do you know what is right for you?

How do you know which way to go?

How can you tell what to choose?

Whether a career path, a healing practitioner, a movie to see or a restaurant to enjoy, **stop** for a moment, **look** around both within and without, **listen** to your heart and your inner Spirit. Then feel, choose, and move with confidence, joy and inner peace.

Our tendency is to make choices based on old beliefs, others' opinions and what seems appropriate or expedient. When in doubt, in fear or contracted, trust that you do not know. When clear, focused, inspired and expansive, choose with confidence knowing there will be success and fulfillment.

The success may be unexpected challenges, healings, gifts, and opportunities. It may be that new options will emerge, as you begin to move forward. You may be fulfilled by offering a gift of yourself to someone you meet. Fulfillment feeds you soul.

There is no wrong way to go. The Spirit of Love within you will use everything for good as long as you suspend or forgive your limiting thoughts and negative judgments. To stop, look and listen within for your Inner guidance will lead you on a path to experience happiness, wholeness and freedom.

Yours To Do

I am willing to take action whenever I am called .

If you see something that needs to be done, it is yours to do!

Whenever we are complaining about something left undone or needing correction or renewal, we have work to do. The public bathroom, rude service at the store, dishes left undone, car unwashed, button missing, someone looking unhappy, etc., all are calls for loving attention.

The one who sees what needs attention is the one who is to give the attention with love.

Sometimes we are to clean up the mess and wash the dishes.

Sometimes we are to respectfully request help from others.

Sometimes we are to let those in authority know of the need.

Sometimes we are to change our attitude and bless the situation.

Whenever and wherever you are called to loving service, listen within your own heart and respond with willingness and gratitude. Forgive and erase all judgments on what you see and you will clearly hear what is truly your part.

It takes all of us together to build a better world.

You Know What is Best

We know what is best for us!
It takes courage, faith and willingness to commit
and choose what is good for our whole and Holy Selves.

Do you love your whole Self unconditionally?
Do you take exquisite care of your whole Self?
Do you deserve the best?
Do you forgive Self-doubts, Self-criticisms and Self-denial?
Do you listen within yourSelf and honor what you hear?
Do you trust yourself to be honest and responsible in Self-care?
Do you know that what is best for you is a gift to others?
Do you remember to love yourSelf as God loves you?
Do you give yourself what makes you happy and healthy?
Do your respect your mind and body and Spirit?
Do you recognize that you make a difference in your world?
Do you realize you are teaching your world by your example?
Are you willing to love, honor and cherish yourSelf today?

**The only mistake we ever make
is when we forget to LOVE.**

Loving your whole Self perfectly is a gift to everyOne!

Feeling Down?

When you're feeling down and blue,

there's just one thing for you to do:

Appreciate the world you see.

Find someone to love and fill with glee.

You know you are the choosing One

who turns the lights on and shades the sun.

You can find the Son (Sun) within.

Listen with heart and you will grin.

For all the beauty around you

is your Love shining through.

More and more you'll come to know,

it is the Love that gives life glow.

With your praise and compliments

every thing makes perfect sense.

When in your gloom preoccupied,

you only see with darkened eyes.

So wake up now and choose again,

give your "thanks" and you will win

The prize of faith and hope abound

as you work and play on Holy Ground.

Spirit within and joy shining out,

now you see what life's about.

Love in all you say and do

gives life meaning and purpose true.

Loving You

Loving You is your first priority!

Can you look in the mirror and genuinely smile at who you see?

Can you get a glimpse of the powerful being you are meant to be?

Can you recognize that loving you is really loving me?

Can you look at your life and your loves and feel great glee?

My intention with these Loving Reminders is to set us free

to really see Who we can be by loving Thee and feeling glee.

Whimsical and wise, carefree and caring, hopeful and confident, challenged and trusting, honest and respectful, assured and reassuring.

This is what I share when I dare to love you and me with the same authentic devotion and passion for the power of our Oneness in Love.

Begin where you are.

Love the Beauty of your Soul.

Enjoy the Goodness in your Heart.

Appreciate the Creativity of your Mind.

Where you cannot love, enjoy and appreciate, clean house.

It is your responsibility to clean up what is not valuable.

Everyone loves, enjoys and appreciates a clean house!

Freedom and Trust

I love You and I know You love me, too!

Love is Freedom!

The freedom for You and me to be who we are.

The freedom to live life as we do.

The freedom to make mistakes and learn from them.

The freedom to express our own truth as we see it.

Love is Trust!

The trust that there is a constant flow of love no matter what.

The trust that, in spite of life's problems, we believe in and support each other's right to live as we choose.

The trust that in adversity there is healing and learning and gifts of love.

The trust that under conflict and emotional expression, there is always love.

I love You.

I trust You.

I free You to be all You Are.

And I receive All I give for mySelf.

I choose to freely trust and give the Love I Am.

Prayer for Remembering

May I ever remember the Truth of Who I Am.

For I am Your Gift given to the Earth and all men.

I am here to be forever Your Loving Reminder,

The One Who remembers and gives Her Holy Self in Love.

May I forever speak Your words and sing Your songs.

May I live in the Your Grace seeing You in each One's face.

May I forever be like You with Your wisdom and Your grace.

Knowing the Perfection of Your creation in all I see.

And when I come to dark spots and bumps in the road,

May Your Truth lift me up and lighten my heavy load.

And when my friends are troubled and seek comfort from me,

May I give them the Love I have, given perfectly from Thee.

You are my Redeemer, my Comfort and steadfast Friend.

You are my steady Guide, my Peace until the end.

For I have chosen wisely to let You Light my Way.

You are the Joy I find within to brighten every Day.

I love You more dearly, as I know Your love for me.

I see You more clearly, as I follow patiently.

I follow You more nearly, as I come to trust Your Voice.

And I know Your Holy Presence. You are my Eternal Choice.

Reminding You

In times of imbalance, hold on to something.

In times of darkness, seek the light.

In times of fear, find someone to love and reassure .

In times of loss, fill yourself with hope and possibility.

In times of pain, be gentle and quiet.

In times of heaviness, let go and detach.

In times of conflict, search for solutions where all win.

In times of turmoil, put things in order.

In times of fatigue, relax and take your rest.

In times of confusion, ask for clarity.

In times of hunger, feed yourself nourishment.

In times of sorrow, let your tears be released.

In times of need, ask for what you really want.

In times of forgetting, ask One Who remembers.

In times of resentment, learn not to expect.

In times of loneliness, be someone's friend.

Life invites us to do what is natural. Be as innocent as a child and you will know how to care for yourself in troubled times. God is natural.

Life can be easy. Love can be safe. You can have fun.

We are all in this together. Let us keep on reminding each other of what is simple and what is true. Then we will not forget for long!

Realize the Love

How can we be active participants in remembering and realizing the Love we are and the Love that Is?

Forgive the apparency, the illusion.

Forgive the eyes that see the awfulness.

Forgive the mind that holds the doubt.

Forgive the heart that lives in grief.

Forgive ourselves for forgetting God is in charge.

Release our hold on tragedy, that keeps us in the dark, so we do not see what is Real and what is True.

God loves me and God loves You.

And so it is with what we know.

Let go of all that is not wholly true and wholly loving!

Judgment and fear stop the flow and hold in place what only appears to be so. Forgiveness and trust open the flow and allow the release so we can see the Son (sun) shining again in our world. Forgiveness heals and makes happiness.

Prayer: May my mind be healed so that I behold the Light and extend the Love of God in all circumstances. I now choose perfect trust in Divine Love and the Highest Outcome.

This I prayerfully and consciously choose and so it is.

The real work is always an inside job. For when the mind is healed (returns to its natural light-filled state), our inner kingdom of peace and joy is out-pictured (made manifest) in our world.

Only love prevails, for only Love is Real.

Effective Clearing

"Good morning!" And so it is, a Good Morning!

Whatever is expressed with heartfelt intention instantly becomes our experience! What a creative opportunity to explore this possibility. For you begin to recognize the importance of your vision, passion and faith as essential to the personal creative process. In truth, any doubts or skepticism of your creative potential is merely offering you direct feedback of the obstacles in your way. So welcome their appearance and then dissolve the inner resistance with conscious forgiveness.

This is **HIGHLY EFFECTIVE.**

EXAMPLE: "I am a beautiful loving presence and I make a difference in my world."

INNER DOUBT: "I am definitely not important. Usually I don't even love me, so how can I really matter."

CLEARING: "I forgive myself for forgetting to love Who I Am.

I forgive myself for diminishing my significance.

I am a beautiful, capable and contributing person.

My loving presence is essential for a loving world."

Begin today to clear your own consciousness and intention and become aware of the amazing shifts, both inner and outer.

Are You Willing?

What is your Will ?
What do you intend to be for You and Your World?

Are you willing to choose consciously for the Highest?
Are you willing to know what to do and where to go?
Are you willing to be the One to shine like the Sun?
Are you willing to speak Love's True words?
Are you willing to learn and to live life fully ?
Are you willing to embrace and remember Love?
Are you willing to be All That You Are?
Are you willing to cherish your Self like a Child?
Are you willing to forgive and forget the past?
Are you willing to be here and now enjoying it All?
Are you willing to give what you have?
Are you willing to listen to your heart?
Are You willing to let Love lead the Way,?
Are you willing to lay all fear gently aside?
Are you willing to heal with your peace?
Are you willing to know Trust resolves everything?
Are you willing to celebrate God's Love for You?
Are You willing to know You are God's Light and Love?

Are You Willing?

Never Quit

Life looks, feels, sounds different depending on what our current filter or perception seem to be. Life can be friend
 or foe, depending on which way we choose to go.

To see clearly after a tremendous storm, we need to clean up, release, purify, forgive and heal. Acknowledge everything we are feeling, positive and negative, loving and hateful. Accept it All!

To know where we are when the dust has settled, we need to look around and appreciate our assets. Explore and acknowledge all that we still have within us and around us. Appreciate the Goodness!

To remember our direction, we must ask our heart what we REALLY want. Make a thorough list of all that we desire to have, to be, to do. Be totally honest with ourselves.

To have the dedication, courage and commitment
to move forward , we must be totally willing to choose again.

Say to yourself everyday, "I will never quit on myself.
I am here to succeed no matter what!"
Have confidence in your willingness to begin again.

Choose Love Instead of Fear

I choose to receive the Abundant Love all around me.

I can be loved for doing nothing.

I extend Love without expecting Love in return.

It is in giving Love that I receive the gift of Love I Am.

Whenever I receive Love, I am grateful and fulfilled.

What is not Loving, I recognize as a call for Love.

Whenever I notice the call, I extend Love joyfully.

Whatever the question or problem, Love is the answer.

Loving is fun, safe and easy.

I enjoy extending Love.

I forgive myself for withholding Love.

I forgive myself for trying so hard to be right.

I forgive myself for trying to be perfect.

I forgive myself for thinking my Love is inadequate.

Love is always received no matter how it looks.

Love always works! Love heals and blesses.

Love sometimes is action and has words.

Love sometimes is still and silent.

The Essence of my Love is always enough.

I trust in Love. I release all Fear.

I love giving Love.

Love always returns to me as I recognize the Holiness and Wholeness in Me.

Afraid of Not Being Loved

When we are afraid of not being loved, very often we seek ways to get attention, a sense of belonging and security. We look for the ways to get what we think we want. Love, **conditional love**, based on our ability to perform or achieve, to care for or stay out of the way, to be naughty or nice, to be attractive or needy. We learn successful ways to achieve conditional love when we are very young by watching the "Love-givers" and caretakers to see what is affirmed, noticed and rewarded.

Some questions to ask yourself: What makes you special? How do you know when you are really valued by another? What do you believe you need to do or give or be or have to "get" the love you want? How will your life be different if you relinquish the need to be special?

Loving Reminders: You are Love Itself. You are created by Love for the purpose of loving your creations and your Creator. To love everyone exactly as they are is to see everyone as a loving creation being loved by you. To love with no conditions is to see everyone and everything with Divine Mind. Life is learning to love unconditionally, to love no matter what.

When we release our need and desire to have a special place on Earth or in Heaven, we realize everything we are is perfect. And we relinquish our faulty attempts to be recognized and loved. We rest in Divine Love and protect this rest by loving All equally, including ourselves.

Saying "Thank You"

"Thank You" means so much more
Than those two little words can say.
"Thank you " means "I love you",
Shared in this simple way.

"Thank you" says, "I trust you"
And will always call you my friend.
My "Thank you" gives you great respect
As our sharing will never end.

"Thank you" is our greatest gift,
true gratitude for all we do.
"Thank you" is the song we sing
Being in this world, me and you.

"Thank you" is the price we pay
As we give ourselves to love.
"Thank you" must be our mantra
For the abundant lives we have.

Say "thank you" liberally. It costs nothing and means everything. Saying "thank you" even to those who seem to push your buttons, for they wake you up. Remember the gift of love is often given with just those two little words.

Follow Your Heart

Are you willing to see and know what your life is really for? Are you ready to accept that you are important? Are you willing to let go of your self made wishes and attachments to what your little self needed and wanted? Are you ready to trust the bigger picture which knows your heart and hears your inner call for happiness and peace of mind? Are you willing to step through the door of defenselessness and allow the light within you to lead the way? Are you willing to imagine that there is no punishment, only forgiveness, for your errors along the way? Are you willing to trust there is a Power greater than you that serves your highest good at all times? Are you willing to let go of your resistance and at least listen to the calling of your heart? Are you willing to love yourself enough to give yourself this gift of Goodness, Wholeness and Beauty?

Start by saying and writing:

I am willing to allow my life to be guided for the Highest Good.

I forgive myself for resisting and limiting my Self.

I am now willing to be listen for the calling of my heart.

I am willing to trust that I am good and my goodness serves.

I choose to say "Yes" to my inner call

I choose to fulfill my purpose here on Earth.

I believe God's Will is happiness for me.

I am willing to be whole, happy and free.

Never Too Late!

It's never too late to say "I'm sorry."
Never too late to begin again.
And never too late to write, "I love You."
Never too late to make a new friend.

It's never too late to give a blessing.
And never too late to say, "Good-bye".
It's never too late to try an adventure.
Never too late to learn how to fly.

It's never too late to heal your childhood.
And never too late to stop asking "Why?"
Never too late to offer forgiveness.
It's never too late to let yourself cry.

It's never too late to reach out to someone.
And never too late to show that you care.
It's never too late to give what really matters.
And never too late to be kind, if you dare.

It's is never too late to know your Real Essence.
And never to late to be Who You Are.
It's never too late to offer Love's Presence
It's never too late to shine like a star.
It is never too late for You. Your world is waiting!

Giving and Getting

The paradox of giving and getting:

To Spirit getting is meaningless and giving is everything.

The cost of giving is receiving.

Giving and receiving are One.

What you give to another, you have given to yourSelf.

Life is for giving. And You are the Gift.

To give your Whole Self freely is to know Who You Are.

Your worth is not established by what you do or make or teach or give. Your worth is established by God.

Your Father's Will for you is Happiness.

You can't take it with you. So enjoy sharing it now!

Happy is the man/woman who has given all his treasures for the glory of God.

Having rests on giving, not on getting.

Trying to "get" leads to regret.

Daring to give is the freedom to live.

You are the Gift

What is my greatest gift to my world and the people I love? First, **I must first know I am a gift**. I must appreciate and value the gift I am. Second, **I need to take good care of this gift**, not overuse or misuse the gift I bring (not take it for granted). Third, **I must give the gift of myself where I am wanted and received gratefully**.

Life is for giving and you are the gift. It is only in giving the gift you are that you recognize the gift you give. Appreciate and take good care of yourself. Give your gifts of self where you are valued, where you make a difference. When you know your giving matters, you are fulfilled. Sometimes the giving becomes an exploration. What do I want to give? What do I have to give? What can I joyfully give? What matters to me? What will set me free to be?

I know for me, personally, I must be happy and healthy to freely give the Truth of my Being, the best of mySelf. I also know I must value and care for the Real Me, impeccably. Then, I must discern (listen within) to know where and when and to whom to give my Self (where I will be received with Love and Joy).

I want you to know, you are a gift to me and I receive You with joy and gratitude. Take care of your whole Self and be happy and at peace. This world needs You and loves You.

Remember to give where you are called, where you make a difference. And know this is Good.

How Love Looks, Speaks and Acts

How does Love act?

How does Love speak?

How does Love look?

Is Love always "nice" or comfortable?

Is Love always meeting the expectations of others?

Does Love look appropriate or fit in?

Does Love always speak with affirmation and appreciation?

Is Love always received with openness and gratitude?

Does the ego enjoy authentic expressions of Love?

If Love is Who We Are, can we camouflage our True Nature by being off course?

If Love is our True Nature, what does it take to remember and find our way again?

If Love is our Path, how do we meet with ego, error, falsehood, arrogance, violence?

If Love is our Calling, do we walk away, deny, speak up, ask for joining, pray, or pretend?

If Love is to be given to everything unlike Love, is it always extended gently and sweetly?

If Love is our Gift, do we give what we believe in and trust?

Do we right the wrongs?

Do we speak to the silence?

Do we volunteer to assist?

Do we ask for accountability?

Do we express what we believe?

Do we seek loving action?

Do we care beyond our words?

Do we look at other positions?

Do we listen to inner guidance?

Do we dare to be contrary to the popular?

Are we willing to "rock the boat" or "stir the pot"?

Do we see beyond the surface?

Do we forgive and forget?

Do we turn our backs on the unkind and unfair situations?

Do we withdraw our love from what is "fear"?

For me Love is courageous and bold.

Love is daring to trust in the Highest Outcome.

Love is risking belonging and popularity, comfort and being nice, to freely express what we see and experience and what we envision and desire.

Love is feeling, wanting and willingness.

Love is authenticity and availability.

Love is strong and true.

Love is willing to work through all things to find a place of appreciation and respect.

Love Is

Love creates goodness and wholeness.

Love heals.

Love sees what is.

Love forgives what isn't.

Love enjoys and appreciates.

Love is peaceful and happy.

Love is helpful and trusting.

Love sets us free.

Love joins with Love.

Love is respectful and response-able.

Love cooperates and harmonizes.

Love chooses with Love.

Love gives freely and lives abundantly.

Love extends and radiates.

Love warms and soothes.

Love grows and nourishes.

Love transforms and enlightens.

Love inspires.

Love endures.

Love succeeds.

Love remembers.

Where is Love hiding in you today? Where can you extend more of the Love You Are? How can you teach your world to Love?

Are you willing to bring your Love to everyone?

Life is Working

How do you know if the path you have chosen is working?

How do you know when to change?

I love myself. I take good care of myself.

I trust myself. I know what is best for me.

I respect myself. I always give myself the very best.

I listen to myself. I take time to hear how I feel and what I think.

I honor my choices. I believe in the choices I make.

I forgive my mistakes. I easily erase, release and choose again.

I know what I want. I support myself in having everything that I really want.

I believe in my life purpose. I choose to be whole and happy and free.

When you can easily say and know that this is true, you will always be loving you!

Use these affirmations to clear the mental and emotional blocks you have learned from faulty thinking and negative experiences.

You deserve the best.

So live the best and forget the rest!

Being Responsible

Who is responsible for the shirts that came from the cleaners with the sleeves un-pressed and with wrinkled cuffs?

Who is responsible for the car left unlocked at the body shop and the radio missing?

Who is responsible for the crumbs on the counter and the dishes in the sink?

Who is responsible for the carwash just paid for and not working and no refund?

Who is responsible for the theater tickets ordered and reserved for the wrong night?

Who is responsible for the promises made and not kept?

Who is responsible for the quality of food we buy at the grocery store?

We know how many times we, being nice helpful Americans, just let it go, do it ourselves, change stores or brands without saying anything, use it any way, think it's all we deserve or never even notice because it is what we're accustomed to receive.

To pick up after our children or our roommate, to take responsibility for another's unconsciousness, to be afraid to speak up, to accept with "That's the way it is these days", to let it go because we don't have the "time" to follow up is our lack of responsibility.

Are we not responsible for creating guidelines and consequences for the behavior of our children? Are we not responsible for teaching ethics, values and common courtesy to our family members and those with whom we interact? Are we not responsible for returning products of poor quality? Are we not responsible to say "Stop! This is inappropriate."?

Are we not responsible to talk to the manager or supervisor or write the company? Are we not responsible to see that the quality of life improves? Are we not responsible to respect ourselves enough to speak up and command respect for ourselves and our neighbors?

If not me, then who? If not now, then when? To be responsible or not, that is the question!

Am I too lazy? Am I lacking confidence? Do I think it unholy or not nice? Am I afraid of conflict? Do I just want the other's approval? Do I hope it will get better if I just ignore it?

I believe if each one of us would be accountable for the agreements we make and take responsibility for our mistakes, we could change the consciousness of humanity. First I begin with me and then I can easily request others to be accountable and responsible, too.

Impeccable living requires consciousness, respect and responsibility. Are you willing?

Upsets

When you are bumped, upset, or your buttons are pushed, there is always a gift. Ask first, " Is this a gift to wake me up to change my attitude, my behavior, my relationships, or my beliefs?" If so, you have been given the opportunity to see where you are holding a position which is not highest and best for you and others.

If not a gift for you, then why would you be hurting yourself with figuring it out, shutting down, worrying about or in anyway taking the message personally? Many messages given are simply and completely for the messenger. When you hear a song or read a story that is not your truth, your work is to let it go, so the messenger can really hear their own truth.

"Thank you for sharing." will be your genuine response in both cases. If you have a 'button', be glad that it gets pushed so you can forgive and erase it from your belief system. If the gift belongs to the giver, you need do nothing more that not take it for yourself.

When anyone criticizes, judges, blames, or gives advice for any reason, they are always talking to themselves first. Sometimes it belongs to the recipient as well. But sometimes it must be left with the critic. So I take the criticism and advice I give very personally. It is always mine!

Be grateful for all honest communication.

What We Sow, We Reap

What we seek, we find.

What we intend, we experience.

What we focus on, we increase.

What we resist, we keep.

What we want, we have.

What we give, we receive.

What we teach, we learn.

What we value, we grow.

What we fear, we strengthen.

What we believe, we see.

What we ingest, we become.

What we become, we express.

What we know within, we give without.

What we think, we create.

To be abundant and prosperous, define what you want.

Identify the wealth you already have.

Make room for your current new desires.

To be rich in what you want and abundant with what you value now, choose again.

To realize the abundance of your unlimited creative self, give what you want to have.

The world is our rich garden. We are the gardeners.

It's about Time!

No time for gossip.
No time for TV.
No time for trivia,
Meaningless novelties.

No time for worries,
No time for tears.
No time for furies
Or needless fears.

Plenty of time
To answer Joy's Call.
Plenty of time
To find Love in All.

Time for Reminders
And moving meditation,
Expressing gratitude freely,
And healing inspiration.

There's time for my family
And for You, if you call.
There's time for God's message:
See the Goodness in All.

There is always time to do what I love. Because time is a resource and a treasure to give, I cherish my time and I use it well with consciousness, clarity, commitment and choice.

The Game of Life

Past, Present or Future, it matters not.

It's all the same what our creator hath wrought.

Some of us dwell in the past grief and regret,

Things we don't want to forget.

And some of us love to future "trip",

Anticipating adventures or fearing we might slip.

And some hang out in the here and now,

Trusting our being or not knowing how

We're going to make it through another day.

See, each of us has our own special way

To learn who we are and explore how to play

The game of life.

With toil and strife or the fun, safe easy way?

Multiple choice with variations, too.

Each of us choosing what we want to do

And where to go to find the answers

That bring our peace of mind.

Listening

For 23 years, I have spent daily time listening within and writing what I hear. My time in nature, my time with clients and family is inner listening. The only times I turn it off is when I **think** I know what is right and wrong, when I have an opinion, or am afraid and try to take protect myself.

I believe all of us are born with this ability to listen within. We lose it when we start pleasing others by listening to their "right and wrong", being obedient to the voices of authority. We literally lose our inner hearing, and then seek outside opinions for answers. With just a little willingness to take the quiet time, we can regain our inner hearing and can feel guided from within. I highly recommend you take the time to get deeply acquainted with your whole and holy Self.

I use my loving reminders as an excuse to stay in touch with me and my inner reality. I am being reminded for myself and for those with whom I share. I love the reminders. Whatever comes up when I write is always applicable during the day in some way. **I feel alive and focused, creative and centered when I open and write what I hear and know from within.** There is no hesitation. Usually the whole message is totally spontaneous, typed as if I were speaking without hesitation. Sometimes there are songs or poems, but usually it is just simply flowing through my life in total trust and freedom.

What a way to really live abundantly and joyfully!

How Do we Know?

So how can we know what is truly from our Inner voice,

Our Higher Self, the Spiritual Guidance, that lives within each one of us?

There is a calmness, a sweet peace and neutrality. In our gratitude and willingness to follow what is for our Good, we hear the inner call more clearly. We can trust in this inner direction, for here we are supported in fulfilling our life's purpose, and our soul's urge to learn and explore. Here we find true rest.

Feel free to gently lay aside possibilities, ideas, beliefs, careers, relationships, and environments as you become aware that they no longer serve You. Your life is yours to choose. Ingest the best and forget the rest. Bless your past choices, right or wrong, good or bad, knowing that they no longer serve you, as you release them and choose again.

Whenever you hear or read anything which is not "right" for you, simply lay it aside. You need use no energy to explain or justify your choices. Simply choose that which resonates with your own inner Voice.

Trust in the choices you make for your Highest Good and the Good of All!

Be Authentic

To be Real is to be authentic and express fully who You Are.
Who are You really?

You are not what others expect you to be.
You are not what you wish you were.
You are not what your parents hoped for.
You are not what can be described or defined.
You are not a diagnosis or a label.
You are not better than everyone else.
You are not worse than anyone else.
You are not the same as anyone else.
You are not the same as you were yesterday.
You are not what you will be tomorrow.
 So who are you?

To be real is to honor exactly who you are.
To be authentic is to respect the way you are right now.

This moment is the only moment for you to be You.

Touch Someone

It's the human touch that counts,

The touch of your hand and mine,

That means far more to the fainting Heart

Than bread or cheese and wine.

        Author Unknown

This poem inspired a talk I gave as a teenager to my church.

And from time to time I remember its simple, poignant message.

And today I reach out to touch you and feel us connecting heart to heart.

I know of no greater healer than our abiding faith and love for one another.

Sometimes one touch, one smile, one word makes a life-changing difference.

Sometimes we spend a lifetime of encouragement, mentoring and confidence-building.

Sometimes we come together briefly for forgiveness and healing and then go on our way.

Sometimes a poem or song, a speaker or teacher lifts us to greater possibilities.

All make a lasting difference and transform our lives forever.

May the meditations of my heart and the words that I write touch you.

Anger

What are the lessons to be learned from having anger expressed both within and without. It looks like there is a reason for being upset and angry. Anger is energy that is withheld until it explodes or is released abruptly without a clear goal. This energy is sent forth with the unconscious desire to blame or make someone feel guilty. Often, we release anger only when we can hold back no longer. Toxic thoughts are expressed with a need to heal and be free of fear or pain.

What is the underlying function of anger and conscious energy release? We know unexpressed thoughts and feelings fester and become toxic over time. We know that energy, "emotion", is meant to be moving and flowing all the time. We know that **love attracts everything unlike itself to be healed**. Love attracts fear and hurt and anger in order to offer forgiveness and healing.

With consciousness, **all our thoughts, words, emotions and actions are designed to create what is good, beautiful and holy.** We know that when anyone expresses what is "not love", they are always calling for love. We know that **to forgive is to see things differently**. We know that **only our thoughts can hurt us**.

As we love ourselves, we are willing to transform all negative experiences into positive opportunities to heal our past fears and self-doubts and remember our own wholeness and holiness.

The way we handle anger, ours or another's, can strengthen and reinforce the Truth of Love. When we remember Love is Who We Are, we respond to all expressions of anger with compassion, willingness to "flush the cosmic toilet",

true forgiveness, and a clear desire to be truly helpful. Therefore, there is no need to "eat" the other's negativity, but rather to assist in the total release. Never let someone's emotional sickness make you sick! **Use your spiritual awareness to offer healing and release**. Take nothing negative personally.

Anything unworthy of God is unworthy of You.

The lessons to be learned by all or any One of us are all the same. We are here to remember: **Love is Who We Are. There is nothing and no one to fear. We can never quit on Love, unless we temporarily forget our whole and Holy Purpose.** In remembering this Presence of Love, we can afford to laugh at all fear thoughts.

Remember, **what others think of you is none of your business**. And when they are feeling unlike Love themselves, they may go to the most light-filled person to help them remember.

Be Love and you will see Love and the call for Love.

Life is simple.

Love is responsive.

Be willing and able to respond to the call for Love.

Everything Matters

It matters what thoughts you have when you change a baby's diapers.

It matters how you treat your hotel room or a friend's guest room.

It matters what you think when you look at someone who is physically challenged.

It matters when you pick up or leave trash in a park or the restroom.

It matters how you take care of someone's creation: a new house, a car, a dress, a meal.

It matters what you say about me when I am not there.

It matters how you treat your family and friends.

It matters when you are grateful or angry.

It matters when you take good care of yourself or ignore your own needs.

It matters what you eat and wear, what you read and think, what you say and do.

It matters what you throw away and what you keep.

It matters what you forget and what you remember.

It matters how you trust and set free, or doubt and hold back.

You are making a difference

You and I matter!

Trust in Good

Changing your mind makes the difference. Your mind is making up what it wants to believe all the time. The thoughts of the observer affect the outcome of the research. Your mind and mine are creating experiences in our bodies, our relationships, our careers, our finances and our world all the time. Every thought creates a result. Every action generates a responding reaction. So it is with thinking.

When we are doubting, scrutinizing, and comparing our lives and accomplishments, we lose the experience of our gifts, our perfection and even our spiritual direction. Giving ourselves appreciation and trust in the purpose of our lives, opens the door to see the goodness, beauty and wholeness that really is there. From birth to transition, all of us are on our sacred journey following the calling of our hearts. Everything really is in our own best interest and does work together for our good.

To trust in the good outcome is to experience a good outcome. And to doubt the possibility or believe in your lack of worth is to diminish your willingness to see beyond the apparency. Most human perception is short-sighted and limited by human beliefs, past experience, judgments and fears. With "love" colored glasses, we see the love beneath the surface illusion.

Creative solutions come from knowing that abundance, wholeness and magnificence are guaranteed by the conscious spiritual knower within each one of us.

Philosophy of Life

Humans have always wondered about the world and its origin, the meaning of life and our relationships with one another. We have time and energy to wonder and listen, when we are not consumed by fear and survival and questing and needing something we imagine we don't have.

What is your philosophy of life?

Do you live your beliefs?

Do you have a purpose in the greater plan?

Do you actively and consciously choose to live your purpose?

If you had a mission here, what would it be?

Are you dedicated or forgetful and lazy?

What really matters most to you?

Do you let life's temptations and distractions mislead you?

When you are tired, afraid or angry, how to you find your center again?

What do you spend your time and energy and money on?

Do you live what you value?

I see how much we are each a product of those influences

to which we have been exposed. It is wonderful to see how it all comes together with no one right or wrong.

Each perspective is whole in and of itself.

Beliefs Made Real

Whatever we believe is "true", our mind gathers evidence to prove itself right. The mind is like a magnet which attracts to itself proof that its opinions are correct. The more judgments, historical beliefs and prejudices we have, the more limited our thinking and our perceptions. What we believe, we perceive. And what we perceive strengthens our beliefs. We literally get stuck in our limited thinking and our false beliefs.

As we undo our false beliefs, misperceptions and limiting creations, we awaken to the Truth of the Original Blessings of Beauty, Innocence and Abundant Love. To see clearly and awaken to the light within, we must forgive our beliefs. Selectively we can access and erase our individual learned beliefs as we discover them. Or we can choose to program our mind to easily and gently erase all that is not of God.

I now choose to forgive and let go of all that is not wholly true and wholly loving.

My mind and body easily erase everything that is not God's Will for me.

I now create and choose thoughts and experiences which are Good, Whole and Beautiful.

I naturally unlearn everything that is limiting, lacking and belittling.

I choose to see the Beauty and Perfection of the Original Creation.

Love & Gratitude are The Giving Way

Give with Joy and you shall receive Joy.

Give sparsely and you shall receive sparsely.

Give freely and you shall receive freely.

Give periodically and you shall receive likewise.

For as you give, so shall you receive.

Notice how and what you are receiving and you will discover your innermost "giving" ways.

Forgive your errors in giving and choose again to give to others, to your world, to your Self and to God as you want to receive from others, your world, your Self and God..

Generosity & Tithing are The Teaching Way

Give always, in all ways, to what you want to teach your world. Give your attention to what you want to strengthen in your life. Invest your resources of time, energy, money and talents to what you want to increase in your universe.

Giving to poverty and lack, yields more poverty and lack. Contributing to education and jobs yields more choices and self-sufficiency. Feeling sorry for, and giving handouts to, the homeless teaches separation and victimization. Find ways to educate, strengthen, and empower your fellowman.

Giving your Self—your time, energy, money and love—in joining to build homes, hope and opportunities, creates joining and a better future together.

Giving gifts, because you should, teaches you and others to do your duty.

Supporting the places and people that inspire you, motivate you and remind you of your freedom, magnificence and abundance, generates an increase in all you desire to be and remember.

Life is a circle.

What is given is received.

Are you seeing, serving and believing what you want to experience in your world?

Giving creates.

Life is a Garden

Life is Your Garden. Whatever you plant will grow. Whatever you remove will be gone. With your kind attention and loving intention, your garden will flourish. With your neglect, impatience, unconsciousness and judgments, your garden will not become what you may truly desire.

It is yours to choose. What is the garden of your choice? Beautiful, bountiful, joyful, useful, playful, simple, dramatic, ever-changing? You are the creator of this garden. It is with your thoughts and your imagination, your words and your affirmation, your activities and your attention, that your life will become what is truly your heart's desire.

And with your denial, your neglect, your regret or blame, your life may represent your own inner negligence, ignorance, self-criticisms, fears or resentment. What we imagine within our own hearts and minds in relationship with our lives is out-pictured in our apparent life experience. So it is important to love ourselves and imagine our lives good and beautiful and wholesome.

It is worthwhile work to erase negative and limiting pictures with forgiveness and positive affirmation. "I deserve and am willing to have a bountiful and beautiful life rich with adventure and contribution to my global family." Now write your own affirmation. Be willing to "Cancel" any thoughts which are not what you want to experience. Be willing to affirm, both written and spoken, what you want to experience over and over. (Some say to write and say each affirmation 20 times daily for 14 days to clear all contrary messages.)

The real value of affirmation is to recognize and erase the unconscious negative thoughts which seem to show up in our life garden as weeds or drought or pestilence and blight.

Bad weather may be negative emotions. Drought may be limited inspiration and attention. Weeds may indicate neglect or allowing negative distraction to take hold. Pestilence and blight may mean that you let go of your own conscious choice. It is time to say, "Be gone" to those influences which are not in your best interest.

All of us are deserving of beautiful gardens which nurture our souls. Pay close attention to what makes your heart "sing" and brings out the best in you. The signs are clear when you look for them. When you find the path of your heart, the way is made fun, safe and easy to enjoy the garden of your life. Remember: Your life is for giving and You are the gift. So love, honor and cherish the gift you are. Your life will love, honor and cherish you right back!

Life is a "Fail-safe" Learning laboratory!

- We all get out of this earth classroom Whole and Holy, no matter how it looks or feels!
- The outcome is sure, and our experience is varied.
- Everyone passes to the next level.
- There is no grading system or ranking of students.
- We can choose to explore and experiment or be cautious and watch.
- Learning happens no matter what choices we make.
- Freedom to learn through pain or joy is our individual choice.
- The only mistake we ever make is when we forget to love.
- We always have the eraser of forgiveness to correct all mistakes.
- Penalties and punishments are self-imposed. and the corrections needed are to release ourselves from judgment.
- Some students play at life; others work hard. Everyone learns. Some earn awards and toys and lots of money. Others just enjoy life. Some students wait until graduation to be free. Others live free. Some students share their learning. Others keep it for themselves Some students praise the teacher and learn easily. Other students condemn and ignore the teacher. They struggle to learn.

This "university", called life, can be really fun, and feel totally safe, and flow easily with enthusiasm and confidence.

It is All Our Choice!

Is Love Special?

Do you earn Love?

Do you give Love just to the Special people in your life?

Are You a gift of Love remembering the Love in everyOne?

A simple way to begin to watch your Lovingness grow is to look at your most genuinely loving relationship. Look for how you think, feel, act and talk around the beloved.

Do you need your child, spouse or friend to be responsive?

Do you look for what you get back?

Is there some intrinsic reward in the giving?

Now imagine giving that high state of unconditional love to everyone you encounter, everyone you think of, in the future and in the past?

How will your world change if you love everyone equally and unconditionally?

And if you loved God unconditionally, how would your life be different?

If God is Love and God is Everywhere, then You Are Love and You are Everywhere. And if God's job is to Love Everyone Unconditionally, your Real Job must be to Love EveryOne.

The question may be, how does God Love?.

God trusts us and sets us free.

One

Chi, Qi, Prana, Ki,

Spirit, Vital Force, Great Mystery,

God, Life Energy, Allah,

The One,

All the same.

One as One.

Where Love grows,

There Chi flows.

Where Chi flows,

 There Joy grows.

God is wherever we are.

And wherever we are, God Is.

We are One with Spirit.

Spirit is One with Us.

Look within to discover Who You Are.

Listen within to know Why You are here.

Led by Your Inner Voice

What if, in the process of inner listening and trusting in your inner knowing (the same as a natural infant and child does), you know and honor your knowing? You naturally know when to eat, to sleep, to eliminate, to create, to play, to work, to give, to receive, to be, to extend, to express, to explore, to move, to rest, to be.

I call this spending my day **flowing with my inner knowing. Trusting myself with no evaluation or self consciousness, simply allowing what is to be fully enjoyed and realized.**

Give yourself a day every month where you allow yourself to flow with whatever your inner knowing calls you to do. It may feel awkward or uncomfortable at first, but in a 24 hour period, you will find some elements of your natural rhythm. Or go backpacking or camping alone, with no time piece and no one to measure your activity. Simply enjoy each present moment and notice where you are led minute by minute. Or choose to begin each day with: "What is my Creator's Will for Me? Where am I to go? What am I to do? What am I to say and to whom?" Let your day (one day at a time) be led by your inner voice, and watch the miracles of love emerge!!

Divine Love or Human Love?

Divine Love, Unconditional Love is Eternal and never-changing.

Human love or conditional is temporary and changes with the people and circumstances.

Unlimited and Expansive Love is natural and the Essence of Who We Are.

Limited and selective love is a protective device coming from our forgetfulness.

Divine Love sees Perfection and is Joyous.

Human love sees with evaluation and is emotionally volatile.

Divine Love is freeing and trusting.

Human love is possessive and cautious.

Divine Love flows with the humans' changing nature.

Human love is disturbed by the personality and behavioral changes in relationships.

Unconditional Love forgives All things.

Conditional love judges and evaluates all things.

Divine Love gives and extends for the Joy of It.

Human loves seeks to "get" something in return.

Divine Love gives All to All.

Human love gives to those in good favor.

True Love is fun, safe and easy.

Learned love is serious, scary and complex.

Divine Love experiences Union, Sameness and Oneness.

Human love experiences independence, differences, and separation.

Divine Love is patient, peaceful and kind.

Human love is pushy, argumentative and manipulative.

Divine Love seeks the Highest Good for All.

Human love seeks personal happiness and satisfaction of its own needs.

I am truly loving You and All.

What If?

What if this really is Paradise?

What if our self judgments are keeping us in hell?

What if our forgiveness could give us heaven now?

What if we are covering our eyes so we cannot see the Light?

What if this is our testing ground to see if we have the faith to believe our Creator loves us?

What if we cannot see the beauty because we are focused on the ugly?

What if our own choices keep us from knowing and owning the Bounty here on Earth?

What if we ourselves create our own problems?

What if we are comfortable with the way it is and afraid to see it differently?

What if we use our minds and our histories to blind us to the Truth?

What if there is nothing to do, but forgive our doubts and fears and see the Love?

What if what we believe is really creating our total experience?

What if Jesus came so we would realize we do have Unlimited and Abundant Life?

What if in our guilt and blame, disappointment and despair, we refuse to believe in Heaven?

What if this is our opportunity to choose again?

What if, by listening within rather than to our minds, we can avoid pain?

What if there really is Holy Spirit or angels always guiding us to the fun, safe, easy way?

What if life really is for giving and we are the Gift?

What if we are afraid to be responsible, and want to blame someone else?

What if our willingness to forgive, listen within and trust God will give us Heaven Now?

Are You Awake?

To be awake is to know freedom.

1. The freedom of choice to be and do and have what your heart truly desires.
2. The trust to listen within your whole and holy Self and honor your own inner calling.
3. The courage to reach out with love in times of apparent need, when there is fear, anger, pain, and distraction.

To be awake is to know trust.

To be awake is to know God.

To realize God, the Infinite, the Omnipresent, the Eternal is present in every aspect of creation, in every one of the human family, no matter what their religion, their choices, their history, or their level of awareness.

To be awake is to know peace.

Everyone has a part in God's Plan.

God's Will is our happiness and to know and live our part in the Divine Plan is our happiness.

Are You Awake?

Enlightenment Is Now!

What is it you seek in life? Is it possible that what you really want, you already have? Could it be that where you are going is a destination without a distance? Let go of the search and experience what you have with gratitude. Stop, look and listen to the reality of now. Perhaps this is enlightenment!

In the endless striving, improving, expanding, planning, desiring, and acquiring, are you not denying and distracting yourself from what already is? Once you notice and enjoy the blessings of today, the gifts expand, you enjoy and appreciate more, and your blessed world increases. Sometimes it seems all that hides the beauty of reality is our endless focus on how it isn't here.

Stop, look and listen. Stop the mind chatter, the incessant denial of love and goodness and wholeness. **Look** into the face of God, the face of Nature, the Great Mystery of Infinite life, with joy and delight. Be unafraid to see your likeness and image in everyone and everything. . **Listen** to the music, the trees, the breeze, the birds, the voices, the laughter, the songs, and especially, listen to your own heart.

Everything in life is an opportunity to discover heaven here and now. The blessings already are. Give up whining and wishing, hoping and praying and start celebrating you and life. **Acknowledge and be grateful for all you have, all you do and all you are—for the gift of your Self.**

Love No Matter what

No matter what the question, the answer is always LOVE.

LOVE no matter what and Goodness prevails.

No matter what the need, TRUST in Divine provision.

TRUST no matter what, and perfect provision is the outcome. No matter where we go, the destination is always FREEDOM.

FREEDOM from fear,

FREEDOM to choose again,

FREEDOM to explore and express.

Thank each one of You for BEING and DOING and HAVING whatever you choose.

Our lives are gloriously intertwined as One.

I am honored and blessed to be here again and again, in Love with Trust and Freedom as my Guides.

I Am in Love's Service.

Simple Truths to Remember

- We are created by Love, as expressions of Love for the purpose of Loving.
- Love is unlimited in Power and in Peace, and therefore, so are we.
- Life can be fun, safe and easy when we think with the Unlimited Mind of Love.
- Everything we think and say and do teaches everyone everywhere.
- Awareness with non-judgment is healing and opens the way to remember our wholeness and holiness.
- We are here to create what is good, beautiful and whole.
- We are here to remember the Love we are and to return to our natural state of wholeness.
- The only mistake we ever make is when we forget to Love.
- Life is forgiving. You are the gift. In giving the gift of your Self, you realize and enjoy the gift you are.

Betty Lue Lieber, PhD, MFT

Our Co-Mission

- **Walk in Faith**

- **Speak with Love**

- **Give with Joy**

- **Live with Gratitude**

Affirmation of Life

May my life be a prayer, a sacred request for all Beings to be whole and happy and free.

May my life be a song—a melody of exquisite beauty and grace, realizing the harmony in diversity.

May my life be a meditation—a silent walk through the marketplace, offering blessings of gratitude and gifts of loving kindness.

May my life be a dance—freely flowing with the inner music of my joyous heart and touching the souls of my global family.

May my life be a gift—wrapped in the awakening colors of Remembrance and opened to reveal the glorious light within every willing receiver.

May my life reveal the love story of God's Glory expressed through every human experience and expression for all time and eternity.

I am glad to be alive.

So Be It and Amen.

Betty Lue

Prosperity Prayer

We are here to be truly helpful.

We give ourselves freely to Spirit, allowing our joyful service to lead the way to gratitude, generosity and prosperity for All.

We allow our lives to be a model for equality, community, contribution and co-creation.

We choose this heart-centered ministry as a way of life, leading us individually and collectively to freedom of expression, generosity of Spirit and the Joy of Abundant Living.

May it be so as we affirm "YES" to co-create what is good, beautiful and holy for ourselves, our community and our world.

Amen.

Creator–Comforter–Guide

Mind–Body–Spirit

Thank you for this new day of Infinite Possibility and Freedom of Choice.

May I have the clarity and wisdom, compassion and courage to:

- Listen to my Inner Guidance.
- Follow my Soul's calling.
- Honor God in All life.
- Enjoy all that I do.

May I walk in God's grace, creating beauty, goodness and wholeness with every thought, word and deed.

As I live each day in Divine Love, I give thanks for gentle opportunities:

- to forgive and heal,
- to live and learn,
- to play and create.

With gratitude and joy, I commit each day to:

- Love unconditionally
- Serve from the Heart
- Remember God

Blessed Be.

In love, we are not afraid.

In joy, we are not stuck.

In peace, we are not alone.

Betty Lue Lieber, Ph.D.

Born August 16, 1942 in Michigan

Living in Hidden Valley Lake, California

Holy Union, life partner with Robert Waldon since 1985

Mother of two daughters + step daughter and son.

Grandmother of eight

Spiritual partner, guide and mentor to hundreds.

Founder of Reunion, Forum for Global Holistic Spirituality

Founder of 20 Counseling-Healing Centers in 5 states

Director of Reunion Living Ministry Program

CA Licensed Marriage and Family Therapist since 1977

Whole Life Coach and Success Consultant

Natural Health Counselor

Feng Shui Practitioner/Teacher

Certified T'ai Chi Chih Teacher

Ordained Interfaith Reunion Minister

Co-Minister of Unity Center for Inspired Living

Doctorate in Theocentric Psychology

Masters in Clinical and School Psychology

Betty Lue's Teachings as a Child

We are whole.

We are not lacking or limited.

We are here to be helpful.

We are happy.

We are loving.

We are free and unrestricted.

We need no criticism or praise. We are right with ourSelves.

We are trustworthy and trusting.

We are honest and open.

We are generous and share everything of value.

We value what is real and lasting.

We are patient as we learn from everything.

We are to love everyone equally.

We are to follow Love and our Inner Truth.

There is nothing to fear.

There is complete innocence as all are children.

there is nothing that cannot be forgiven.

All paths lead to Good.

All things are possible.

Love gives us everything we ask for in the name of Love.

Miracles are natural.

We are all in the family of man and everyone is our brother.

God is Love and we are His loving creation.

Healing comes from the release from guilt and fear.

Reunion Ministries

Reunion Ministries was a gift from Spirit for me and those I have worked with over the last 35 years. This non-profit church without walls, organization without requirements, programs without evaluation, spirituality without dogma, is a forum for all to explore their own beliefs, to heal their hearts and open to Spirituality within their own lives. These precepts are the guidelines through which we grow together in Trust and Freedom, the essence of Love ItSelf.

Precepts of Reunion

We are all Spiritual Beings.

All life is inter-connected.

Love is our natural state and the unifying force of all creation.

To create what is good, beautiful & whole is our call.

Forgiveness and freedom from judgment and fear bring healing and love.

All relationships bring us into conscious awareness of our blocks to love and our healing needs.

We are here to learn & teach what we are learning.

We respect all Beings, honor all Paths.

We listen within and serve the Highest Good for All.

Reunion:

A Forum For Global Holistic Spirituality

Reunion offers the space of freedom & trust in which to:
1. Reclaim our True Self.
2. Actualize our full potential.
3. Balance our relationship with all life.
4. Live our vision of cooperation and co-creation.

Mastery of Reunion

My intention is to inform, inspire and invite you to join with me in whole life integration and inner REUNION.

1. *Align mind, body and Spirit.*
2. *Honor heaven and earth.*
3. *Balance home and work.*
4. *Explore real work and recreation.*
5. *Give yourself quiet & interactive time.*
6. *Realize connectedness with all life.*
7. *Accept human differences.*
8. *Respect all life.*
9. *Know harmony and unity, inside and outside.*

This is truly the mastery of Inner Reunion.

Betty Lue Lieber, PhD, MFT

Betty Lue Offers

Consultations:
By phone, Skype, email, home or office.
Phone: 800-919-2392 voicemail/pager
Email: bettylue@reunionministries.org
Home: 17664 Greenridge Rd., Hidden Valley Lake, CA 95467
Offices:
Reunion Center for counseling, Healing and Growth
3496 Buskirk Ave, #103 Pleasant Hill, CA 94523
Unity Center for Inspired Living
50 Sand Creek #140, Brentwood, CA 94513
Positive Living Center
17568 Spruce Grove Ext, Hidden Valley Lake, 95467

Reunion Living Ministry Program
See ReunionMinistries.org

Experiential training for those who seek to focus and facilitate their spiritual development, life purpose and calling.

Workshops and Retreats— See ReunionLakeHouse.org
Email your request for annual schedule of retreats.

Daily Loving Reminders
Receive by email—*bettylue@reunionministries.org*
View on the web at *www.lovingreminders.org*

.

Books published
Loving Reminders
Peaceful Reminders
Relationship Reminders
Pocketbook of Affirmations
Healing Reminders

Coming soon
Family Reminders
Healthy Reminders
A Child's Reminders

Give Your Self to Love

&

Love Will Give to You

Betty Lue Lieber, PhD, MFT

www.ingramcontent.com/pod-product-compliance
Lightning Source LLC
Chambersburg PA
CBHW071455040426
42444CB00008B/1354